CW01658660

LION'S PRIDE: THE TURBULENT HISTORY OF NEW JAPAN PRO WRESTLING

LION'S PRIDE: THE TURBULENT HISTORY OF NEW JAPAN PRO WRESTLING

Chris Charlton

Copyright © Chris Charlton 2015 All rights reserved
'Lion's Pride' shield design is © Dave Barlow 2015 All rights reserved
Cover design © Aya Charlton 2015
Photography is property of AFLO and respective photographers. Used with permission.
Reproduction or redistribution of this book's text or imagery without written consent of the author is strictly prohibited

This product is in no way endorsed by, or affiliated with, New Japan Pro Wrestling, Bushiroad, or any other corporate entity or individual.
www.lionspridebook.com Twitter: @lionspridebook, @reasonjp_

ISBN-13: 9784990865818
ISBN-10: 4990865812

For Louis

Prologue: Wrestle Kingdom Come

Photo: Yukio Hiraku/AFLO

On January 4 2015, 36,000 wrestling fans filed into the Tokyo Dome to watch Wrestle Kingdom 9. It was actually the 24th consecutive time New Japan Pro Wrestling ran the country's largest sporting venue on the same date for their biggest show of the year. 2015 was different though; more eyes, with a broader reach were on this event than ever before.

Through a new subscription streaming service, NJPW were pushing technical boundaries few in the risk averse Japanese sporting or entertainment industries had dared to challenge, allowing viewers worldwide access. Meanwhile, the company was making their debut on North American pay-per-view channels, with English commentary provided by Matt Striker and the legendary Jim Ross helping viewers through a very different interpretation of the medium casual American viewers had become used to.

As Hiroshi Tanahashi pinned Kazuchika Okada in the main event, retaining his International Wrestling Grand Prix heavyweight title, there was a positivity around NJPW not seen in a long time. Its stars were breaking into the mainstream, attracting product endorsements and appearances on prime time talk shows. Merchandise from shirts to trading card games was selling strongly around the globe, and most important to the company's bottom line, live tours were consistently selling out.

All this sounds like the ending to a fairytale movie of NJPW's history. Here, it appeared, was a relatively small company that could, rising to top-level status domestically and abroad. In truth though, the story of New Japan Pro Wrestling isn't one of rags to riches. WK9, in fact, was a highlight in an ongoing journey to redemption. NJPW, like wrestling at large in Japan, started out as a spectacular phenomenon, but didn't always maintain that high, as poor decision-making and financial mismanagement almost sank what was in some ways a national institution. This is the story of the rise, fall and rise again of NJPW, as the King of Sports lost and regained its crown.

1

Japan's National Korean Icon

In Europe and the United States, professional wrestling rose out of humble beginnings, born in working men's clubs and travelling carnivals. The medium, discounting failed introductions in the late nineteenth century, had a much more auspicious beginning in Japan.

The nation was in the grip of the US occupation post World War 2. While western economies boomed, national morale was low as citizens tried to recover lives impacted by years of firebombing and two nuclear attacks. Food and luxury goods were strictly rationed, leading to a surge in organized crime, as yakuza quickly capitalized by selling goods on the black market.

Sports were used to raise national morale; affordable live entertainment allowed the public to regain a sense of pride in their nation - a nation now constitutionally bound to peace. Baseball was one such sport, and some seven decades later it remains enduringly popular. Pro wrestling was another, and arguably the most strategically sound American export for the time. What better way of instilling national pride in the public than by giving them the chance to see homegrown heroes show their physical superiority over the occupying westerners? Wrestling's (still, naturally, staunchly protected) predetermined nature ensured Japanese talent would shine, and entranced crowds would leave happy.

The burgeoning Japanese wrestling scene would be built around two figures who had achieved success in other martial arts: legendary judoka Masahiko Kimura and accomplished sumo wrestler Rikidozan.

Born Kim Sin-Rak, Rikidozan's birth and early years in what is now North Korea would ordinarily preclude him from being a Japanese national icon. Training as a sumo wrestler in Nagasaki prefecture (the site of the second American nuclear attack on the country at the close of World War 2), he was tormented because of his race. Korean immigrants and their descendants still suffer from racial discrimination in modern day Japan, and tensions were significantly higher in the 1940s, a short while after the country's annexation by Japan in 1910. With the knowledge that success in sumo would never be granted him due to his birthplace, Kim Sin-Rak would renounce his Korean nationality, change his name to Mitsuhiro Momota, and claim Nagasaki as his adopted home town.

Much as in pro wrestling, sumo wrestlers normally have ring names, or *shikona*, assigned to them by their stable masters. Re-re-christened Rikidozan, Momota attained considerable success - a 135-82-15 record garnering him the rank of *sekiwake* in 1949. Yet frustration with what he saw as institutionalised racism within the sport saw Momota leave sumo. *Sekiwake* is the highest rank a sumo wrestler can receive on merit alone; access to the two divisions above it is based on tournament performance and the discretion of the sport's governing body. For Momota, there was a clear glass ceiling imposed by a nationality he couldn't cleanly erase.

Pro wrestling was a chance for Momota, under the Rikidozan name, to break through the ceiling sumo had imposed. After training with American Freemasons in Japan, he wrestled in Hawaii, before heading to Northern California and Pacific Northwest territories, where fresh wounds from the war made him an easily hated heel. By the time of his return to Japan, Rikidozan, through print and broadcast media that was attracted to the idea of a Japanese athlete fighting the oppressive Americans, had constructed a new patriotic persona for himself.

Forming the *Nihon Puroresu Kyokai* (lit. Japanese Pro Wrestling Association, or JWA) with funding from friend Nick Zapetti (a noted mobster credited with introducing western practices of organized crime to the Japanese yakuza), Rikidozan populated the nascent sport with imported American talent for him to beat in singles or tags with the aforementioned Kimura. These not only brought fans in their droves to arenas, but saw crowds amass outside electronics stores to watch their heroes triumph on the prohibitively expensive televisions on display. Rikidozan in particular was propelled to stratospheric levels of fame, and his popularity was extremely lucrative to the JWA and the yakuza king-pins that circled after the business' clandestine cash. It was a profitable trip for touring Americans like Lou Thesz, too, who were eager to relive Rikidozan's battles in the American territories with the nationalistic baby-face/foreign heel dynamic flipped.

Outside the ring, Rikidozan became a movie star, appearing as himself in a handful of films through the mid 1950s, and even a recording artist. Mindful of his past however, and with an opulent lifestyle suddenly granted to him though his success, Rikidozan was a heavy drinker, and a paranoid figure. Fiercely protective of his spot at the top of a business he saw him-self as creating, Rikidozan was not at all keen on the idea floated by JWA's money men of feuding with former partner Kimura on an even footing. The plan was for a December 22 1954 match between Kimura and Rikidozan, the country's first heavily promoted all-Japanese main event to crown the inaugural JWA champion, to end in a 60 minute draw, and the two to be embroiled in a feud through 1955 that would see Kimura's star rise to Rikidozan's level.

Not long into the bout, and with what seemed like little more than an errant kick from Kimura striking Rikidozan slightly below the belt for provocation, the former sumo wrestler interpreted it as a vindictive move and promptly lit into the judoka with a brutal series of palm strikes and kicks to the head. A stunned Kimura had no answer, and was knocked out by the back of Rikidozan's hand. Rikidozan was Japan's first major wrestling champion, but with Kimura's planned star making performance ending in him being beaten to a bloody pulp, the self proclaimed father of Japanese wrestling had made powerful enemies.

Thesz/Rikidozan packed out Korakuen Stadium, predating the Tokyo Dome *Photo: Nikkan Sports/AFLO*

For now however, Rikidozan was on top of Japanese pro wrestling and the public consciousness. The JWA was a hot ticket for the rest of the '50s both as live event and early television attraction. In more recent years WWE television will struggle to pull a 3.5 television rating in the States. A 1958 Rikidozan/Thesz NWA title match drew an 85 - *eighty five* - rating, a remarkable achievement even given the apples to oranges time period comparison. During his run at the helm of JWA, Rikidozan would also train prospects in Tokyo, among them Shohei "Giant" Baba and Kanji

"Antonio" Inoki, who will become big players (to put it mildly) as our tale continues.

It was the star's dealings with Japan's underworld that did him in, meanwhile, and this wasn't just limited to the Kimura incident. Rikidozan opened nightclubs in yakuza territory controlled by gang boss Noboru Ando, leading to the mobster plotting to have him murdered and to kidnap three other JWA headliners. Ando would abandon the plan, but Robert Whiting's biography of the aforementioned Nick Zapetti paints friend Rikidozan as a figure who was increasingly on edge - sleeping in hotels with that evening's live gate in cash and a loaded gun.

On December 8, 1963, Rikidozan was partying at a club in Asakusa. He headed to the restroom, where he was stabbed by Katsuji Murata of the Sumiyoshi-Kai yakuza syndicate. There are conflicting reports over what happened next; some say he continued socializing with guests before receiving treatment (indeed this is the version of events depicted in his 2006 biopic) while others say he went to a local hospital where he was treated for a minor wound and sent home.

Indeed, the knife wound was minor, but the blade Murata used had been soaked in urine. Days later, Rikidozan was dead, a result of acute peritonitis. The JWA was thereafter run by committee in the place of the adopted national icon, and resulting power struggles would see the promotion split into two major groups.

2

New Beginnings

After a brief hiatus, JWA started 1964 with a series of shows at Tokyo's Riki Sports Palace (named appropriately enough, given the passing of its former leader), most headlined by the tag team of Toyonobori and Yoshinosato, taking to the ring against Cowboy Cassidy (under his 'Mr. Civilian' character) and 'Killer' Buddy Austin. That Japanese babyface team comprised two of the four stars who stepped up and took the reins in the day-to-day running of JWA after Rikidozan's death.

Toyonobori, real name Michiharu Sadano, shared Rikidozan's sumo background, entering the sport as the JWA was gathering popularity in the mid '50s. Upon leaving sumo, he was trained by Rikidozan, and would be part of a tag team with the JWA founder in the lead up to his death. Toyonobori was now President of JWA, and Yoshinosato, another sumo wrestler turned pro, was Vice President, leading to the pairing billing themselves as the promotion's top two stars.

Under these two was Yoshimura Michiaki, a junior heavyweight who had a successful run in rival promotion All Japan Pro Wrestling Association (not the AJPW that would spring up later) before being scouted by Rikidozan after AJPWA went under in 1956. He would be an accomplished supporting player in JWA, and over the next few years would win several All Asia Tag Championships in different teams, including with the aforementioned Toyonobori, and with both Antonio Inoki and Giant Baba.

Finally was Kokichi Endo, who was a judoka before being trained by Rikidozan and debuting with JWA in 1954. This would result in another student/teacher tag pairing in addition to Endo also tagging with Toyonobori, Yoshinosato and Baba in the years to come.

The four steered JWA through the rest of the sixties, but by the end of the decade, disputes between Toyonobori and his three co-directors would see the first dominoes of JWA's collapse start to wobble. As is often the case in pro wrestling, finance and ego were at the heart of the split. While Toyonobori was in his mid-thirties and therefore still in his prime, there was debate behind the scenes as to who should represent the company's next wave of stars. However, Toyonobori's pick to join him in the main event mix differed from that of the other three, the ensuing spats leading to the former sumo star's expulsion.

Kanji Inoki was born into a wealthy Yokohama household in 1943. After his father's death, his family ran into financial hardship, which eventually led to their emigration to Brazil. In his high school years in South America, Inoki was a standout athlete, and he was noticed by Rikidozan when promoting a card in São Paulo in the spring of 1960. Inoki was invited back to train with Rikidozan, and seeing the potential of appealing to a South American audience (Brazilians make up one of Japan's largest expatriate communities thanks to strong bilateral relations after World War 2), JWA would bill him under the name Antonio.

In the early '60s, Inoki worked in a number of semi and main event six man tag matches with teachers Rikidozan and Toyonobori against foreign heels like Killer Kowalski and Karl Gotch. After Rikidozan's death, Inoki publicly announced his fully Japanese roots, and headed to tour America shortly after JWA's restart in March 1964.

Usually under the billing of Tokyo Tom, Inoki worked in Los Angeles and Texas, and formed strong relationships with contemporary stars - his tutelage under Rikidozan helped him start a relationship with Gotch that reaped rewards a decade later. He returned to Japan in 1966, and Toyonobori instantly wanted to make him JWA's top star.

By this time however, Toyonobori's influence as president had eroded under the combined power of Michiaki, Endo and Yoshinosato, who already had their favourite, and weren't going to let their golden boy relinquish his spot to the returning Inoki.

Shohei Baba was a natural rival for Inoki from the outset, so much so they could easily be protagonist and antagonist in a *Tiger Mask* style manga. They both chose wrestling instead of a promising sports career, though Baba outdid Inoki, staying in Japan and making the big leagues for a time, pitching for the Yomiuri Giants baseball team before quitting the sport after an elbow injury. They enrolled in the JWA dojo a mere one day apart, and one can imagine Inoki and his classmates feeling downtrodden. Due to Baba's size and relative celebrity status, the imposing 209cm man was allowed to commute to the dojo for training instead of sleeping in the cramped, sweaty gym with everyone else.

To further paint Baba as Inoki's mustache twirling nemesis, the pair debuted on exactly the same day, September 30, 1960. Inoki was in a losing effort, which has always been typical booking practice for newcomers to Japanese promotions; there's early emphasis on lessons in humility for the young talent, and dues paid with the audience who can see the progression of a young star. Baba, meanwhile was given a victory in his first outing, a rare occurrence indeed, and not against a fellow neophyte either; Yonetaro Tanaka was a part time worker for the most part, but a veteran bit-part player of six years at this point.

Inoki found himself outdone at every turn, with art imitating life in the ring as well, keeping him at a lower rank than Baba. In the handful of times Baba and Inoki squared off against one another between 1960 and '63, Baba won every time (in fact, Baba usually came out on top in all of his matches, except when in the rarified air of Yoshinosato and other JWA high-ups).

When Inoki returned to Japan, he saw a JWA where Giant Baba was working highlighted matches, including a bloody two out of three falls brawl against Fritz Von Erich (the Japanese babyface had now transitioned from fighting for national pride against oppressive Americans to fighting for national pride against goose-stepping German stereotypes played by

Americans). There didn't seem to be a prominent spot spare for Inoki, and his biggest advocate in Toyonobori was being forced out of his presidency over political differences with Yoshinosato, Michikai and Endo.

Toyonobori sought to start his own promotion to rival the JWA, and appealed to Inoki's ego. If Inoki returned to his former promotion, he'd be just another body, while Yoshinosato had a stranglehold on the main event and Baba was the golden boy that crowds were thronging to see. With Toyonobori, Inoki would have a promotion built around him, returning from America as Japan's biggest prodigal star since Rikidozan.

However, Toyonobori's Tokyo Pro Wrestling neither seriously rivaled JWA, nor propelled Inoki to massive heights. Inoki was indeed headlining the group's first show, against Johnny Valentine, but the new promotion had a sore lack of talent. Toyonobori's student Masa Saito showed promise that would eventually come to fruition in the decades to come, but he was too inexperienced at this point, having debuted with JWA a mere year earlier. Similar 'green' ness affected Masao 'Rusher' Kimura's ability to draw audiences.

Another big hit to Tokyo Pro was a lack of foreign talent to establish homegrown stars in international feuds that were still popular nearly two decades after modern wrestling's inception in Japan. Valentine excepted, Tokyo was short on international stars thanks to JWA's affiliation with the National Wrestling Alliance in America. That ensured JWA had exclusivity on everyone with NWA ties from Dick 'The Destroyer' Beyer to Von Erich, scuppering Toyonobori.

Shortly after the first Tokyo Pro card on October 12, 1966, the group was promoting joint cards with another JWA splinter promotion, International Wrestling Enterprise, founded by Hiro Saito and former JWA financial chief Isao Yoshiwara. By 1967, Tokyo Pro was gone, and an embittered (at Toyonobori), and, perhaps, embarrassed Inoki swallowed his pride and returned to JWA.

Once back in the fold, Inoki would spent the next four years steadily emerging from the shadow of his nemesis Baba, by working together with him. Inoki and Baba would form a tag team in 1967 by the name B-I *Hou* (cannon), and the two young stars between them made a declarative statement about the future of wrestling in Japan.

In Fukushima on October 27, the pair won their first of four NWA International Tag Team championships by beating Bill Watts and Tarzan Tyler. Inoki missing a Hiroshima show due to heavy snow in January 1968 necessitated the titles being vacated, but B-I Cannon all but owned the belts until the end of '69, only dropping them for brief periods (the shortest and most irrelevant being for a two day run to Crusher Lisowski and Dick the Bruiser).

The pairing saw Inoki's star rise as a singles performer as well, and he would only be beaten in the popularity stakes by Baba himself. In October 1970, Dale Louis won a tournament in Missouri to crown the first NWA United Nations Heavyweight Champion. Inoki won that belt shortly afterward on a tour of Los Angeles, and brought it back with him to the JWA, which would turn it into a secondary title similar to the IWGP Intercontinental title today.

This coincided with an increase in television revenue for JWA. Up to this point, their cards were televised on *Nihon Terebi* (NTV), but the company had inked an additional deal with the nascent Nihon Educational Television (NET) station. This resulted in an intriguing brand split, several decades before WWE attempted a similar experiment in the US. As a make-good to NTV, JWA agreed that the network would have exclusive rights to flagship cards featuring Baba. NET would air Inoki's matches, including UN title defenses.

Twin television revenue streams were a rare piece of financial good news for JWA during this time, however. Rudderless from a business perspective since Yoshiwara's departure in 1966, JWA was spending more money on touring and bringing across NWA talent than they were making from their own stars and live gates. Inoki grew frustrated; in his mind, a blow-off cross brand matchup between Baba and he would make for a huge payday that would solve, or at least delay, JWA's financial hardships. Yoshinosato et al nixed the idea repeatedly; it was too soon after the brand split, when letting matters percolate would make for a bigger payoff, and besides, there would be no way NET and NTV would come to terms on broadcasting the match so soon after the network compromises.

Inoki was convinced JWA under its current regime was doomed to failure. He began to plan a coup; he talked to friends within the company, and made plans with Baba himself; the pair together would have enough clout to overthrow JWA management. Word about the plot reached higher ups, however. Inoki was fired, while Baba was convinced to stay on. Finding himself in a similar position to Toyonobori five years prior, Inoki was out of a job in Christmas 1971, and hatching a plan to start his own group. He reached out to allies within JWA, convincing the likes of 16 year old rookie Tatsumi Fujinami to leave the company, and sought out figures like Masa Saito, who had been working as an independent since Tokyo Pro's closure.

In January 1972, Inoki held a press conference, announcing the name of his new venture: *Shin Nihon* (New Japan) Pro Wrestling- NJPW.

On the Philosophy and Psychology of Japanese Wrestling

Japan was not at the 'ground floor' of the pro wrestling business, wrestling becoming a phenomenon in the country after its rise in Europe and the Americas. After cards for decades were built around the concept of Japan versus the world, the psychology of a Japanese wrestling match became a strange hybrid of foreign and domestic philosophies, creating a unique viewing experience. A challenge new fans may have in watching Japanese wrestling is the difference in psychology, making a Japanese promotion less accessible than the easily grasped product of WWE for example, with its simple three act morality plays.

Take, for one issue, the babyface/heel dynamic that is the basis for every western wrestling match. The evil heel's job is to cheat or otherwise be despicable in order to earn 'heat' and move the crowd to the babyface's corner. On the face of it, modern NJPW is drastically short on heels. Kazuchika Okada has youthful arrogance as part of his character, yet has crowds mimicking his trademark Rainmaker pose, and buying into manager Gedo's promos, with his energetic delivery and rolled 'r's making him sound like a thug from a yakuza movie. Minoru Suzuki kicks the Young Lions that work as roadies, holding ropes open and cleaning the ring, as he makes his entrance, yet as he does so, the entire audience belts out the chorus to his entrance music, a triumphant '*kaze ni nare*!' ('become the wind'!) in a hair rock ballad.

Without a set and clearly defined babyface and heel, goes western logic, without explicit instruction to the audience as to whom to cheer or boo, why, nobody would bother reacting to anyone! A Taka Michinoku, or Taichi are traditional heels that garner the 'love to hate' reaction western fans expect, but they're undercard acts. The Bullet Club are main event stars that consistently behave as heels, their nature as foreigners and outsiders making them easier to despise (while still being popular at the merchandise table). In 2015 Tetsuya Naito would play a rare top tier Japanese heel, but only after aligning himself with a foreign stable in CMLL's Los Ingobernables. Why does everyone else in NJPW appear, at least up to a point, to be a babyface?

Perhaps it's in large part due to the nationalistic origins of wrestling in the country. Decades of main events saw Japanese babyfaces and foreign heels, and the huge match-ups between top Japanese stars played like 'what if' scenarios that didn't require the added set dressing of a devious opponent. The roots of the medium in Japan lead most domestic promotions to be 'babyface territories' so to speak, companies built around an 'ace' that was established through months and years of consistent victories. In the nationalistic era of pro wrestling they were all conquering Japanese athletes, and when all Japanese main events became more common, it was less a matter of the crowd having no horse in the race, but rather being invested in their favourites regardless of out of the ring conduct.

Kazuchika Okada is a wealthy, conceited and cocky character in interviews, but has rarely been perceived by the audience as an outright heel in his matches with Hiroshi Tanahashi over the last three years. In fact, Tanahashi has often had a heelish approach in wrestling Okada, but there's a genuine interest in which star is superior overriding the 'black and white hats' supposedly being worn.

Whether a wrestler catches on with the audience, then, is less about being all smiles and baby kissing, but more in showing 'fighting spirit', and toughness and expertise under pressure. Unlike in the west, Japan has never fully let go of the concept of 'kayfabe'; while WWE frequently breaks, and redefines the fourth wall of fiction by having babyface Superstars declare their goals of entertaining rather than victory, Japanese cards for the most part are presented and sold as legitimate sporting events, even if the audience is at least vaguely wise to the way things work. To whit, victories and losses carry a heavy significance, and in-ring, a star taking punishment and fighting back is deeply appreciated.

A six month angle ran in the summer of 2014 that centered on a long losing streak for Tomoaki Honma. Yet, in showing fire and in coming so close to victory in strong performances with the likes of Tomohiro Ishii or Katsuyori Shibata, Honma emerged as a solid fan favourite, whereas losing streak angles in the US are rarely successful. A similar level of respect is shown to Ishii, despite his gruff, plain interviews. A mixture of convincing selling and repeatedly aggravating legitimate injuries has cemented him in the upper echelon of talent in fans' eyes.

What of the match structure itself in Japan? Fundamentally things are similar, although with few angles and talking segments in Japanese wrestling, and NJPW in particular, more emphasis is placed on a match to tell a story, and distinctions in character are more subtle. The US philosophy of 'cheating for heat' is largely absent, but transitions in pacing where mat wrestling is suddenly interrupted by a strike or dive let fans know how to react. Crowds have favourites, but will often side with an underdog, even if it means changing allegiance. The best play up to this philosophy. Tanahashi is NJPW's ace, and top babyface in a babyface territory, but often works in a heelish manner to get fans behind the idea of an upset loss.

The underdog's fighting spirit, the idea of a wrestler standing up to heavy damage, often seemingly receiving a shot of adrenaline to withstand a powerful move only to pop up and go on offense, are cornerstones of 'strong style'. NJPW coined the term close to the company's inception. Inoki, along with Kotetsu Yamamoto, have since been identified as its pioneers, as they trained talent in New Japan's dojo. It's often reductively explained as a hard hitting style, where strikes in particular are laid in far more forcefully than in western matches, where grueling travel schedules preclude potentially injurious wrestling styles.

Strong style is really a marketing term that codifies the hybrid style emergent in Japan in the '70s and persists in main events today. Inoki himself was strongly influenced by Gotch, Rikidozan, and Bill Robinson, and most NJPW stars have spent time in Europe and the Americas as part of their journey to the main roster. Strong Style marries the showmanship of American wrestling with the grappling of European Catch, and it's the best of all worlds approach that makes Japanese wrestling so compelling.

Strong style has its tropes though, and isn't safe from criticism. Short cuts to showing fighting spirit often feel like phallus waving; during All Japan's hottest period in the 1990s wrestlers like Mitsuharu Misawa, Toshiaki Kawada and Kenta Kobashi trading elbow shots in a long drawn out slugfest was commonplace, and garnered huge reactions. Used today, it can often get tired when the spot is repeated in a card. Some, too, are seemingly eager to prove themselves in a needlessly reckless fashion; in today's age of awareness as to the dangers of concussions, Hiroki Goto or Tomohiro Ishii unleashing skull to skull unprotected headbutts seems like an odd anachronism.

There's concern too that the tough nature of the style forces a certain old fashioned mentality on wrestlers, pushing too hard inside the ring, and being uncaring of health outside of it. Recently there does seem to be more protection for talent in NJPW; Kota Ibushi missed three months of action in 2014 after a concussion, when he may have rushed back otherwise. Still, this has come at the expense of well being and lives; Misawa's death in the ring at a NOAH event in 2009 could well have been averted had he not wrestled in such a physical manner, especially when in ill health and injured. All Japan star Nobukazu Hirai was assaulted by stablemates backstage after a match in 2011 as punishment for a poor performance; he suffered a stroke in a match shortly after and went into a coma. While freak accidents happen everywhere in wrestling, in-ring deaths (such as the death of Masakazu Fukuda after an errant elbow drop by Katsuyori Shibata in 2000) seem less rare in Japan than elsewhere, and there is an argument for greater care to be granted to talent in and out of the ring.

Tanahashi is at the forefront of a new philosophy in Japan, and as an ambassador for the medium at large in the country has spoken publicly about having a more moderate philosophy, a happy medium between the all out showmanship of WWE and the '*kibishii*' (strict/harsh) older Strong Style. NJPW have even explored different philosophies on wrestling's direction in the ring. Matches with Tanahashi against hard hitting veteran Minoru Suzuki and Strong Style devotee Shibata have seen real disagreements on where wrestling should be headed play out in front of the audience's eyes. The Japanese style is in the process of evolving once more, and hopefully in a way that retains its uniqueness while looking after its practitioners.

3

Talent and Television

The parallels between Inoki at the start of 1971 and Toyonobori in 1966 are obvious; forced out of JWA, both sought to create new companies in their wake with the help of remaining Association allies. Tokyo Pro was a failure, a fact that Inoki was well aware of, having had his career potentially derailed by his sojourn there. If he was to prevent NJPW from meeting the same fate, Inoki would need two things: (foreign) talent, and television.

A NOTE ON TELEVISION

Major Japanese promotions sell their television rights in a very different way to western companies. While WWE or TNA may shop complete, produced shows to networks in much the same way as dramas or documentaries, Japanese wrestling promotions typically sell broadcast rights to stations, who handle production themselves. The WWE product is essentially the same whether appearing on USA Network or Spike, but NJPW shows are made by TV Asahi or Samurai Network production companies, and announcers specific to the broadcaster, not the promotion. To that end, wrestling is an expensive proposition to a network in Japan, who have to pick up production costs and not just air time.

To compensate, those broadcasters will own the rights to shows aired in perpetuity. This issue came to the forefront in 2002, when an embattled Inoki attempted to sell the NJPW tape library to Vince McMahon as he shored up the WWE 24/7 on-demand service. Asahi forbade the sale, and, scrambling for cash, Inoki would pass the majority of the company to son Simon shortly afterward. The eventual sale of that stake to Yuke's was likely the best all round resolution in the long run.

The problem was that Inoki had neither. Even after Inoki's departure, NET was still in bed with the UN heavyweight half of the JWA as far as television was concerned, and from a talent perspective, JWA also still held the all-important ties to the NWA. Inoki spent the close of 1971 making trips to Mexico and the US in a bid to directly court talent and rekindle his friendship with Karl Gotch stemming from his American tours in the mid '60s.

Gotch was a key, influential ally that Toyonobori had lacked. After being ostracized from most NWA territories after a backstage brawl with Buddy Rogers in 1962, Gotch had plied his trade internationally, and agreed to use his connections to help the fledgling NJPW. Gotch would bring across a handful of American talent for as long as it took for Inoki to find a TV deal.

With a main event of Gotch and Inoki, NJPW held its first event at Oita Ward Gymnasium on March 6 1972, a match Gotch won in 15 minutes and 6 seconds. In every other match on the card, a thin talent roster was bulked up with Gotch's talents (the journeyman tag team the Durango brothers worked with Kotetsu Yamamoto and Toyonobori, whom Inoki had mended fences with, and Ivan Kameroff and Mike Conrad, who had a brief career as the Brooklyn Kid among other gimmicks, also featured) and partnerships struck up in Mexico such as El Furioso, who has, along with Tatsumi Fujinami, the distinction of being in NJPW's first ever match.

The new promotion's Opening Series tour ran fourteen nights over a one month period, with interest and attendance decent, but no TV stations drawn in, archival footage of the March 6 show all that remains 43 years on. Aware of the expense of laying on shows without TV backing, Inoki constantly reassured fans that a deal was forthcoming. Still, though, two more Opening Series tours and a New Summer Series run of shows in

August were only presented to live audiences. Inoki needed a big match to sell broadcasters on and on October 4 presented a main event between himself and Karl Gotch to crown NJPW's first 'Real' heavyweight champion. The new title and chance of Inoki beating his foreign mentor in a star studded match (Lou Thesz, still a draw to Japanese crowds long after Rikidozan's death, was special referee) saw a 10,000 strong crowd sell out Kuramae Sumo Hall, and for the first time, TV Tokyo cameras, which aired NJPW's first television offering at 10:30 that evening. Inoki won the match and the title, but via countout, sending the crowd home happy with a new champion, but cannily opening the door for a rematch with a more decisive finish.

NJPW had some more events in the New Diamond Series aired on Tokyo's Channel 12 in a late evening slot, but a better TV deal would soon come along, thanks in no small part to the declining fortunes of JWA, and the actions of Inoki's arch rival.

As live gates tailed off, and JWA continued to make financial missteps, Nihon Television wanted out of their deal, and Giant Baba was coming round to Inoki's idea of going independent. Baba left, and with his trainees Yoshihiro and Mitsuo Momota (Rikidozan's sons) formed All Japan Pro Wrestling, taking NTV with him, and NWA membership shortly afterward. What remained of JWA was a shambles, with Kintaro Oji and Seiji Sakaguchi remaining as the company's twin stars on NET.

Sakaguchi wanted to merge JWA and NJPW while Oji was determined to keep JWA alive. Sakaguchi left, joined NJPW, and NET cancelled JWA to go back with Inoki, a relationship that lasts to this day, NET rebranding as TV Asahi in 1977. With no TV and next to no talent, JWA limped on for a few more months before folding in the summer of '73, while NJPW started their second year of operations on firmer footing.

The domestic roster was bolstered somewhat with Sakaguchi's entrance, as well as that of his followers to a lesser extent; a young Masashi Ozawa could have been a marketable giant, but was never elevated to a Baba level, instead earning more fame working with Andre the Giant in WWF as Killer Khan.

While the foreign talent being highlighted during 1972 were veterans already established in Japan, 1973 saw Inoki work with a heel of the company's creation. Jagjeet Singh Hans had emigrated from Punjab to Toronto as a teen, and wrestled as a vicious heel against the likes of Sweet Daddy Siki, his wildman, proto-hardcore style earning him the name of 'Tiger' Jeet Singh. After working in featured matches around Canada and the northern US, Singh would debut in Japan on May 4, 1973.

It was a non-conventional debut for a talent in Japan. Singh, wearing a turban, was positioned in the front row of a Big Fight Series show in Tochigi. In the semi main event, as Kotetsu Yamamoto (part of the initial departure to NJPW from JWA, and involved by this point in training talent and booking shows along with Inoki) wrestled Steve Rickard, Singh hopped into the ring and beat down Yamamoto.

Singh, then, was working at the top of New Japan cards from the outset, and later that year, would be shot to a main event program. On November 5, Inoki was shopping with his wife in Tokyo. Singh showed up and slapped Inoki's wife in the face, with a wild brawl ensuing. The publicity stunt was major headline grabbing news, setting up a red hot angle and a feud with Inoki that lasted for years, while starting a career in Japan for Singh that ran for over two decades.

In many ways this was wrestling booking by the book; professional wrestling is always about accentuating a talent's strengths while hiding their weaknesses. By highlighting Singh as a dangerous, crazed individual, embroiled in heated disputes with Yamamoto and Inoki, or by having him enter arenas through crowds clutching a saber in his teeth as terrified fans scattered, audiences were so wrapped up in him as a character, his glaring shortcomings as an in-ring talent were easily ignored, as more proficient opponents carried him through.

As the feud evolved, Singh blowing a fireball at Inoki's face in early 1974, and Inoki storyline breaking Singh's arm in their March 19 match, moves were being made that echoed a lot of the booking decisions made in the wilder, more forward thinking American territories like Detroit or Memphis. America still had a huge influence on Japanese wrestling, whether in New or All Japan, and while Mexican and European influences would see the Japanese style become more of a hybrid, the fact was that nine out of ten cards would be headlined by a Japan v America match.

An all Japanese main event was incredibly rare after the infamous Rikidozan/Kimura match. Inoki would wrestle IWE talent Strong Kobayashi in a cross promotional match in March of 1974 which drew a fair amount of press, but a long term feud with two Japanese stars was all but unheard of at this point.

The symbiosis between Japan and the US saw booking philosophies carry over. In NJPW, this meant out of the ring angles like the shopping centre stunt, as well as matches that were precursors to the Japanese hardcore style of FMW, W*ING and BJW later on. In AJPW meanwhile, working relationships with Verne Gagne's AWA saw a lot of that promotion's shortcuts applied, with non finishes and referee bumps being commonplace.

Inoki and Yamamoto were smart to merge headline grabbing angles with a grounded sporting approach, though, and in April of '74, NJPW ran a series of matches arranged in a league style format. The World League was the first long form tournament in New Japan, setting precedent for the kind of intricately booked (properly booking a large series in wrestling is immensely difficult, as drama has to build over the course of round robin matches towards the final couple of cards where inevitably things go 'down to the wire') tournament that the promotion was always successful with up to and including the always popular G1 Climax summer series of the last two decades.

The month long league was entirely constructed of Japan v America matches, and after round robin bouts, the highest ranked Japanese wrestler faced the most successful foreigner. Inoki would win, defeating Killer Karl Black in the final.

The foreign talent in the World League was present largely as a result of NJPW's relationship with the Buffalo based National Wrestling Federation. The NWF relationship brought across talents like Johnny Valentine to create a Tokyo Pro reunion with Inoki, as well as Puerto Rico talent Victor Rivera, a young Andre the Giant, and the original Sheik, Ed Fahrat, who was an ideal partner for Singh during the Inoki rivalry. Singh and Inoki's matches in '74 and '75 were over the NWF Heavyweight title. Inoki had wasted no time in adding the title to his collection, beating owner and promoter Johnny Powers for the belt a matter of weeks after the business relationship started. Soon enough, Inoki would buy the promotion outright.

Had Inoki had his way in 1973 though, his ever growing trophy case would have included the NWA Heavyweight title. In the summer of that year, Inoki was trying to enter NJPW into the NWA, only to be denied entry because of the Alliance's connection to Giant Baba and AJPW. Eventually the NWA would relent and allow New Japan to be recognized in 1975, but, at Baba's behest, without Inoki himself allowed to be a member with a deciding vote on what happened to NWA championships. Instead Seiji Sakaguchi, who by now had risen to the status of NJPW Vice President, sat on the board alongside business manager Hisashi Shinma, who would go on to have a big hand in the growth of a number of important talents.

Both in and out of the ring, NJPW, and Japan as a whole, spent a great part of the 1970s crafting and marketing a style and brand of wrestling that was more its own, a mongrel breed of European, American and Mexican philosophies. Despite lacking the judo and sumo backgrounds of the generation of top stars before him, though, Inoki had a fondness that bordered on obsession with other combat sports and this would be a distinguishing factor for NJPW over other promotions. More than twenty years before UFC and PRIDE brought the concept of Mixed Martial Arts to the public consciousness, Inoki would dabble in MMA. While his foresight in 1976 could be commended, the expensive failure it created would create a specter that haunted the company later on.

On New Japan and Cross Media

One area where Inoki was far more comfortable and savvy than Baba in the early years of their respective companies was in the use of the media. Expanding the audience of NJPW and reaching a younger and more diverse crowd was a priority, and achieved through a remarkably forward thinking cross media mindset.

While talk show and radio appearances were expected promotional tools, Inoki pushed his brand into new areas, taking risks with mixed results. He and several contemporary stars appeared in 1976's *Pro Wrestling Star Azteckaiser*. A kid's oriented drama, it fell into the same *tokusatsu* (special filming/effects) genre as favourites like *Ultraman* or the *Kamen Rider* shows of today, and much like these staples, is a wonderfully camp watch.

The story centered around the devil himself appearing with his Black Mist group, demolishing superstar Strong Ricky and drawing the ire of 'Aztec hero of justice' Azteckaiser, who would race to save the day on a tricked out tricycle, usually fighting Satanic minions along the way. Once in the ring (after an appearance by the mighty Inoki himself, of course, to insert mild moralizing about doing one's best and so forth), the show changed from a live action presentation to an animated approach, allowing the character to perform some unlikely looking maneuvers. Despite the show generating a three series run of manga books, it was a TV ratings flop, and plans to bring the Azteckaiser character to NJPW shows were nixed. Japanese wrestling had missed out on one of the goofiest characters of all time, but the show's campiness was preserved in laser disc format and now Youtube.

Inoki's first major attempt at creating a cross media star for NJPW was unsuccessful, but if his own character of Azteckaiser was a flop, greater success would be had by licensing someone else's creation. *Tiger Mask* was an Ikki Kaniwara penned manga that ran in the late 1960s. Wildly popular during its three year run, it was successful enough to spawn a televised anime running for over 100 episodes.

Taking some cues from Rikidozan's history, the manga and anime tells the tale of a wrestler that was a despised heel in the United States who returns to Japan, has a change of heart and becomes an adored babyface, fighting for the future of children growing up in the same orphanage where he was raised. Naoki Tsuji's iconic drawings would burn in the minds of many growing up in '60s and '70s Japan, Tiger Mask becoming a universal symbol of pro wrestling to many - observe, for example, the character of King in Namco Bandai's fighting game series *Tekken*.

Inoki was a fan of the series, and elected to license Kaniwara's characters for use in NJPW. Satoru Sayama was selected to play the role of Tiger Mask; after some early matches in a characterless Young Lion role, he had been sent to the UK for seasoning. Here he wrestled under the Bruce Lee style persona of Sammy Lee on World of Sport. 1970s UK was not exactly concerned about sensitively portraying Asian characters, but he was a respected high flying babyface during his European sojourn.

Sayama debuted under the Tiger Mask hood in April of 1981, and that same year, TV Asahi started a rebooted version of the *Tiger Mask* anime (with a bit part, naturally, reserved for Inoki once more). It was a perfect storm, NJPW's network partner giving a platform for the anime that attracted nostalgic fans of the original and younger audiences that loved the character. To add fuel to the fire, British great Marc Rocco, who had worked with Sayama during his WoS days, came in to play nemesis Black Tiger for a feud that really sparked the junior heavyweight division in NJPW.

In 1983, Sayama, tired of backstage politics and the heat from a failed coup of New Japan, slammed the company's fake fighting in a television interview and lead an exodus from NJPW to form UWF Japan. Rather than use a different wrestler to play the role, Inoki, in a strange move, instead sold the Tiger Mask rights to All Japan, while retaining the option to use the Black Tiger character (a Joker without a Batman, this left Rocco no real compelling program to work in Japan, and he would instead portray the character in Mexico for the better part of the '80s).

AJPW would assign the Tiger Mask gimmick to a young prospect by the name of Mitsuharu Misawa, who would play the character until the spring of 1990. Rights defaulted to NJPW thereafter, the mask going to Koji Kanemoto and then current talent Yoshihiro Yamazaki via Michinoku Pro. By this point, memories of the manga and anime had faded, but the character still held its own mystique, a credit to Kaniwara's original work. Speaking shortly after removing the mask, Misawa would comment that garnering a reaction from a crowd was more challenging under the hood; that the audience would expect remarkable superhuman feats from Tiger Mask the character, and give him a harder time than Mitsuhara Misawa the wrestler.

By the time the Black Tiger hood had gone through some bizarre hands (briefly even being worn by the cement headed heavyweight Tomohiro Ishii) to settle periodically with Rocky Romero, its cross media roots were long forgotten. Romero's feud with Yamazaki was built around the latter's tutelage under Sayama, with Romero introduced as a student of Rocco's to present an entirely real-world oriented angle rather than anything comic book-esque. Indeed a 2004 Tiger Mask movie, *Shinsetsu Tiger Mask*, was a biopic of Sayama, rather than the character he played. Sayama actually portrayed his own trainer in the film, as Masakatsu Funaki played Sayama himself. A cinematic reboot of the original manga and anime in 2013, meanwhile, was a forgettable flop. Still, the success and longevity of the character showed Inoki's canniness in NJPW's early years.

Lightning would strike twice when Go Nagai's manga series *Jushin Liger* was aired in animated form on TV Asahi, giving NJPW the ability to license its main protagonist. Unlike *Tiger Mask* and *Azteckaiser*, *Jushin Liger* didn't have wrestling as its inspiration, instead being a tale about a child granted the ability to enter a giant biomechanical suit to do battle with monsters bent on destroying Japan.

Following the Tiger Mask pattern to a tee, NJPW called Keiichi Yamada back from the UK in spring of 1989 to assume the Liger role. Yamada was ending his Young Lion apprenticeship with the UK tour for seasoning, where he had even worked extensively with Marc Rocco, as Fuji Yamada (at least All Star Promotions had the nationality right this time).

While Liger's source material was slickly produced, handled by the same animation studio at Sunrise that produced favorites *Gundam* and *Cowboy BeBop*, his entrance at the Tokyo Dome on April 24 1989 evoked *Azteckaiser* more than anything. Yamada's performance against veteran junior heel Kuniyaki Kobayashi was a sloppy one to boot, but the fans were buoyed by a strong overall product, and hot crowds helped Yamada find his feet in the gimmick and turn in more awe inspiring performances over the coming years.

At Liger's peak, art and life managed to come full circle, resulting in the 1995 film *Jushin Thunder Liger Ikari no Raimei: Fist of Thunder*. This was a camp

Jushin Liger is easily the most successful licensed character in NJPW history
Photo: Yukio Hiraku/AFLO

straight to video *tokusatsu* flick that started Liger as a wrestler rather than super hero. In a shock, the film featured Liger unmasking from the outset, though it was actor Masaru Matsuda, not Yamada, playing Liger himself.

Yamada continues to portray Liger 26 years on from the character's debut, despite an attempt to create an evil Liger counterpart, creatively dubbed Super Liger, flopping with Chris Jericho under the hood.

If Jushin Liger was an example of the popularity of the product helping make an otherwise camp character more popular, and cross promotion seem more organic, Heat was an example of the opposite. With NJPW taking a licensing hit on merchandise sales for Tiger Mask and Liger, Heat was an *Azteckaiser* like attempt to create a cross media star of the company's own, this time via a kid's oriented video game rather than anime or live action TV.

Toukon Heat (the game) was a title for Nintendo's Game Boy Advance system; a role playing game about a young star rising through the NJPW ranks, produced by journeyman developers at PCCW. Heat (the wrestler) was Minoru Tanaka, a junior heavyweight star in an era when junior heavyweights were booked into near oblivion. His shoot-fighting background and legitimate tough guy presentation had given him more believers in management than fellow juniors, and his star was on the rise.

While the GBA had significant cache with kids as a gaming platform in 2002, NJPW as a whole was entering a tail spin. With fewer casual fans than in the 1980s, there were fewer youngsters to buy into the Heat gimmick, and fewer wrestling fans that would be drawn to a game built around him. Tanaka fared poorly in the role, despite a run with the IWGP Junior Heavyweight title, and never seemed comfortable under the brightly coloured gimmick. He quietly dropped the character not long after.

Today, under the considerable media clout of owners Bushiroad, NJPW is more concerned with making the stars it already has span various media rather than adopt a character from another company's intellectual property. Older mainstays like Manabu Nakanishi and Togi Makabe frequently appear on daytime TV in gourmet segments, promoting NJPW as an aside rather than forcing wrestling down the throats of an audience that may not accept it. Makabe would garner the company and himself major attention by providing voice acting work for the Japanese dub of *Mad Max: Fury Road* and subsequent crossover merchandise helped build attention before the 2015 G1 Climax.

More youthful talents make cameos on shows and advertising for Bushiroad's kid friendly card games and associated TV shows like *Vanguard* or *Buddyfight*, which regularly features Kazuchika Okada in cameo roles and commercials. It's a sign of humility not to go back to the well that spawned Liger and Tiger Mask at great risk and expense, but also of cooler heads prevailing, and faith in the talent to sell themselves and the NJPW product. As New Japan's audience skews ever younger, it seems to be working, and bringing with it a new generation of fans.

4

The King of Sports

After Inoki's purchase of the NWF, it had remained in name only as the body fictionally governing New Japan's heavyweight title. To make things more confusing, NJPW itself would now fall under the auspices of the NWA. Before that though, December 11 1975 had legendary British grappler Bill Robinson challenge Inoki for the NWF Heavyweight Title in a gripping two out of three falls match that went all the way to the one hour time limit. The crowd exploded as Inoki locked in his signature Cobra Twist hold at the last minute, but Robinson held on for the draw in a match that announcers hyped as the clash between freestyle and Strong Style.

Robinson and Inoki were firm friends, and Robinson would have a long career in Japan training NJPW candidates as well as successful judoka and MMA fighters. His grappling style, informed by British Catch wrestling, would begin an infatuation among Japanese wrestling connoisseurs with 'Lancashire style', and it, along with the hard-nosed no-nonsense American style of working popularised by Lou Thesz were major contributors to the creation and labelling of NJPW's 'Strong Style'.

As Inoki embroiled himself in angle heavy feuds with Tiger Jeet Singh and The Sheik, he was also determined to protect the business of wrestling in Japan, as skepticism gradually eroded 'kayfabe' in the West. Moreover, Inoki was determined to protect his particular brand of wrestling above all others, and especially that of a certain Mr. Baba. NJPW, Inoki declared, was not merely the king of wrestling, but the King of Sports, a slogan created in early 1976, and still used by the promotion four decades later.

In order to prove this, Inoki himself would spend the better part of 1976 wrestling with top athletes proficient in other martial arts. Creating the Real World Martial Arts Championship, Inoki sought out prominent martial artists to face in worked bouts in order to further establish himself as an all conquering superstar, and his company as the leading brand of wrestling. The end goal would be a June 25 bout with Muhammad Ali, arguably the greatest international sports figure at the time, which would see the boxing great put over Inoki strong with the world's media watching.

The media hype train, and the circus Inoki constructed around himself, whipped into quite the fervour. Ali's English spoken word albums were countered by Inoki's own records, introduced by the song Inoki would use as entrance music going forward, and featuring the chorus of '*Inoki! Bom ba ye!*' a parody of the chants for Ali during his legendary Rumble In The Jungle fight with George Foreman.

Four months before the match, Inoki wrestled Willem Ruska, a judoka with the unique distinction of being the first person to win two judo gold medals in the same Olympic Games in Munich in 1972. Though Ruska, at this point retired from judo competition, would go on to wrestle full time for New Japan for the next few years, he was a complete novice to pro wrestling at this point, and it showed. 10,000 fans were drawn to the Budokan for the bout (which Inoki won via referee stoppage after three consecutive back drops) but were left largely confused by what transpired.

Ruska performed like someone in his first wrestling match, because he was. He moved awkwardly and reacted to Inoki's pro wrestling offense in a wooden fashion. When the match took a grappling turn, things looked more familiar - to a modern day MMA viewer. To a wrestling fan in 1976, even in the less choreographed days of the medium, things looked strange, and without knowledge of why this might be in wrestling's kayfabe days, fans were detached from the match. Sports writers meanwhile, saw the fight as a farce, particularly as the post match saw Tiger Jeet Singh throw a cartoonish fit at ringside and beat up Inoki's seconds. They had dim views over Ali 'selling out' by engaging in a match with a wrestler.

Ali had his reasons to sell out, of course; six million of them. Inoki was willing to grant a massive payday to the boxer to further himself and NJPW; not only was this headline news in Japan, but the June night in the Budokan would also see more international eyes on the company than ever. Via Hisashi Shinma's position on the NWA board, NJPW created an in with Vincent James McMahon's World Wide Wrestling Federation. McMahon would promote Inoki/Ali in the States, airing highlights of the Ruska match on WWWF TV, and taking the unprecedented step of selling a closed circuit airing of the Budokan Ali match as the main event of a card at Shea Stadium in New York, simultaneously beaming that signal to cinemas across America and even in the UK.

Budokan was sold out, and Shea had 32,897 people packing it, just to watch a screen. The event did big business; the problem was that the match was a disaster. The plan pitched to the Ali camp was for a worked pro wrestling match that would conclude with Ali throwing a punch that would strike the referee. With Ali distracted by the errant blow, Inoki would hit his trademark enzuigiri head kick and a recovering ref would count the pugilist out. Inoki would get his win, and Ali would remain protected, but the Ali camp refused to lose a pre-determined bout, in one version of the story at least. in Inoki's recounting of events Ali was expecting the bout would be worked only to be told it would be legitimate, and the boxer was intimidated on seeing Inoki's grappling game in training.

Regardless of the reasons, the two camps were at an impasse, and incredibly, the rules for the bout weren't decided until all the way up to the night before the match. The compromise landed upon was built to fail; it would indeed be a legitimate bout with 15 three-minute rounds. Ali was allowed to take down and strike a downed opponent, Inoki was not allowed to take down Ali (presumably a concession to prevent the boxer having to take a bump), and could only kick his opponent if he had one knee in contact with the mat. The rules were not made public until the bout itself took place.

A farcical 'fight' ensued, Inoki spending the best part of an hour kicking at Ali's shins from the mat on the way to a limp draw that left nobody happy, least of all the people that paid money to see it. A McMahon wouldn't repeat the closed circuit experiment until nearly a decade later, with Vince Jr. running the first Wrestlemania. Like many promoters and wrestlers, Inoki could reverse engineer history in order to further NJPW's King of Sports label to an extent, but he had an audience that had grown a distaste for 'Real Martial Arts'. Ali had gotten his payday, but looked awful, having thrown all of six punches in the match, and worse, receiving twin blood clots in his legs.

There was no doubt that the match was an expensive flop, critically if not commercially. Inoki would face another boxer, Chuck Wepner, in October of '76, and have a rematch with Ruska that December, but the dabbling with martial arts would be phased out, at least for the next few years; unless you managed to peeve Inoki enough to unleash a beating as he did on clumsy Memphis heavyweight the Great Antonio in December 1977.

One upshot of Vince McMahon Sr.'s promotion of the Inoki/Ali fight was a strong relationship with the WWWF that saw a lot of talent move to and from the New York territory, all the way down to Shinma appearing as a storyline WWWF president and working an angle with Andre the Giant. Andre's star was in the ascendancy in New Japan, and the WWWF working relationship also brought Bad News Allen and Stan Hansen into NJPW.

Hansen was fresh off of working with Bruno Sammartino, famously breaking the long time champion's neck in New York before making his Japanese debut in '77, defeating NWF champion Inoki in a non title match. Hansen instantly drew a lot of attention in Japan thanks to his hard hitting style, vicious lariat, and Jeet Singh like intimidating entrance, his cowbell swinging wildman character all the more frightening if one knew Hansen was all but blind without corrective lenses and could easily accidentally clobber bystanders. As we go into the 1980's, we'll see Hansen rise to become the biggest foreign star in the history of Japanese wrestling, though a lot of that legacy comes from his work in All, not New, Japan.

The latter half of the '70s though saw the importance of foreign talent emphasized less in favour of generating home grown stars. This might have been due to financial issues; Inoki was hurt by the substantial payday for Ali after the Budokan fight, after all. Soon there would be a series of talent raids with All Japan, too, and the ongoing war between Baba and Inoki would see foreign stars make a lot of short term money, but ultimately be devalued in environments where bookers felt a star could leave at any time.

While there was undoubtedly a glass ceiling for NJPW heavyweights, Inoki and Vice President Seiji Sakaguchi being the undisputed top two stars in the company, there was an increasingly robust mid card developing. Umanosuke Ueda had developed a unique persona in the more hardcore IWE in the middle of the decade, with a snug brawling style, and a dyed blonde look that stood out at the time (indeed, it would be paid homage to by the likes of Toru Yano much later). He entered New Japan teaming with Tiger Jeet Singh, propelling him straight into a main event deathmatch with Inoki in February 1978.

Strong Kobayashi, a few years after the heavily promoted IWE/NJPW cross promotional bout, had also left the JWA spinoff that had started to flounder, and would be a strong hand in the upper mid card, often teaming with Sakaguchi or Inoki.

There were also promising heavyweight prospects being developed in house, the most exciting being Riki Choshu. Born Kwak Gwang-ung, he had wrestled for his native South Korea in the 1972 Olympics, before being scouted and recruited by NJPW in 1974. With Inoki and company keen to push Choshu hard, he was given the rare privilege of winning his debut match over El Greco with the Scorpion Death Lock (aka Sharpshooter) that he is credited with popularizing. By the end of the 1970s, Choshu had returned from receiving seasoning in America, and was poised to become one of the most important figures in 1980s wrestling.

With a burgeoning roster of domestic talents, NJPW capitalized by setting up the company's first all Japanese tournament, running from November into mid December 1978. The Pre Japan Championship saw six NJPW Stars face off against six freelance talents in a round robin league, before the top eight stars would be entered into a knockout tournament.

The tournament was a backdrop to present a main event with Inoki squaring off against Hiro Matsuda. Matsuda was a former teammate of

Inoki's in JWA, and after that company's demise mainly wrestled in the States. In his brief reappearance in Japan, he would team with Masa 'Mister' Saito in NJPW, before returning to America and being a key liaison between NJPW and US territories, most notably the WWWF. He would also have a hand in training a huge number of western wrestlers, including Hulk Hogan, who would be introduced to NJPW audiences in the early '80s.

The Inoki match was decent, Inoki winning with a Cobra Twist in a bout that would assuage those suspicious that Inoki's charm was solely down to nationalistic pride. As fans chanted his name, Inoki submitted Matsuda as both men's seconds rushed the ring, but neither wrestler was the true star of this tournament.

Inoki and Matsuda had both been granted byes into the knockout phase of the Cup. The round robin league portion allowed talent to shine without the Inoki shaped glass ceiling in place, and highlighted with a perfect win-loss record was a smaller talent wrestling out of his weight class: Tatsumi Fujinami.

Fujinami was just 16 when his trainer Inoki invited him to leave JWA and help form NJPW in 1972. A prodigy, Fujinami dazzled crowds with a higher pace of wrestling and innovative offense, with a full Nelson suplex and sleeper hold with the neck and body bent backwards both named after his 'Dragon' nickname. Shinma arranged for Fujinami to head to New York, where he captured the WWWF Junior Heavyweight title from Jose Estrada.

Fujinami returned home with the belt, which became the de facto major title for the lighter, smaller stars of NJPW. He brought out the best of every opponent during a twenty month reign as champion, whether with middling talent like Ryuma Go, or more promising stars like Satoru Sayama, who along with Fujinami helped define a junior heavyweight breed of Strong Style. The grappling and strikes of Inoki and Sakaguchi were blended with intricate flying spots and rope work being utilized by Mexican luchadores and British light and welterweights like Jim Breaks, Johnny Saint, and 'Dynamite Kid' Tom Billington.

Fujinami's rise to prominence, and increased fan base in Japan and the US was being dubbed 'Dragon Fever', a phenomenon that would see the star relinquish the Junior Heavyweight title to move up to heavyweight in 1981. Sayama would head to the UK and return with a very different character. Choshu waited in the wings, as Inoki was a major nationwide celebrity with a vice grip on NJPW's main events. The 1980s were set to be an exciting decade.

The Ten Most Significant Foreign Wrestlers in NJPW History

Pro wrestling itself being an import, foreign talent has played immense importance to the medium's development in Japan. From Karl Gotch in the early years, through Vince McMahon Senior and Hisashi Shinma, to today's referee and backstage official Tiger Hattori, the role of the foreign talent booker has been an important one in NJPW. The amount and quality of the foreign talent booked in the company meanwhile is often used as a signifier of success.

While the medium's nationalistic roots often paints foreign talent into a heel role, this isn't always the case. Karl Gotch and Billy Robinson's seminal influence on wrestling in Japan would earn them an enduring respect. Stan Hansen and Bruiser Brody were appreciated for their lumpy ring styles, especially in All Japan. Later, Scott Norton would at least be somewhat appreciated by Japanese fans as a perennial, stabilizing figure while dwindling fortunes in the early 2000s meant that fewer foreign talents were being booked.

Obvious language barriers lend an air of mystery or inaccessibility to foreign talent in fan's eyes, and much as with the west, the lack of progressive voices in the creative mix perhaps harms their perception. Too often, foreigners are either one dimensional 'blue chip' athletes that work hard, or are sneaky and brash heels 'gaijin smashing' through promos by brute forcing pigeon English (and leading to an easy pop for the Japanese babyface, who can manage 'I'm gonna kick YOUR ass' from the wrestler's Japanese/English phrasebook). Kenny Omega was a refreshing alternative to that dynamic while working in Sanshiro Takagi's Dramatic Dream Team promotion, being allowed to express himself in Japanese, but this character element would be denied him as a Bullet Club inductee in 2015.

As NJPW moves forward, and with a desire for international expansion, simply bringing fresh faces in the same roles won't do the job; instead, bringing dimensionality and personality to talents on a level of their domestic counterparts will be essential.

The following ten stars, not listed in any order, have had an immense impact on the growing role of foreign talents in NJPW:

'Prince' Devitt

One of two contemporary stars on this list, Fergal Devitt represents the modern breed of foreign talent in Japan. While still in his early twenties wrestling in small venues for Irish Whip Wrestling and the struggling NWA spinoff promotion UK Hammerlock, Devitt moved to the LA Dojo, an initiative started by the Inokis to hunt out foreign talent for careers in pro wrestling, MMA, or both.

NJPW management took pride in the young Irish prospect, and rewarded Devitt's investment in the company with a slot in Jushin Liger's CTU stable in the mid 2000s. As he made his start in Japan, Riki Choshu would be the one to change Devitt's name to Prince, since Fergal would be a mouthful to Japanese fans, and he was too young to be 'King'. He would go on to have runs with both singles and tag team Junior Heavyweight championships, the latter with Ryusuke Taguchi as the Apollo 55 tag team.

Fans, still conditioned to boo foreign talent over domestic stars, embraced Devitt because of his background as an adopted son of NJPW. In 2013, Devitt started to feud with Hiroshi Tanahashi in a series of thrilling matches, with a long term storyline of the junior heavyweight trying to step up to the heavyweight champion and ace of the promotion. While crowds adored Devitt in the underdog position, he would increasingly push the envelope and bend rules, acting increasingly heelish as he desperately tried to prove himself. This slow build to a heel turn saw him form a unit with Karl Anderson, Tama Tonga and Bad Luck Fale, three other Dojo graduates, in May 2013. The Bullet Club was instantly controversial. Miming guns pointed at fallen opponent's heads, and roughing up Tokyo Sports reporters giving interviews led to a level of contempt from the audience rarely seen since the heyday of foreign heels in the '70s and '80s, all under Devitt's purview, who played an evil mastermind perfectly.

Repeatedly scouted by WWE, Devitt left in 2014 still with a lot of mileage in his heel persona, but with time to establish a name in the States running out at the age of 33. As much as the role of Bullet Club member is at danger of becoming a cliched one now, Devitt was remarkable for playing a heel with unprecedented character depth in the group's foundation.

Karl Gotch

This list is not ordered, but if we were to rank the top foreigners in NJPW history, Karl Gotch would be number one. In the early '70s when NJPW was formed, a promotion was nothing without foreign talent, and without NWA membership, it's perfectly reasonable to surmise that Inoki would have no promotion after his departure from the JWA if Gotch hadn't been there for him.

Gotch worked with young talents in NJPW into the '80s, here in his last match with Osamu Kido *Photo: Moritsuna Kimura/AFLO*

Gotch, on the outs with the NWA, worked as NJPW's foreign booker until the promotion finally garnered Alliance membership, and was also willing to work numerous main events with Inoki on early New Japan cards. Gotch already had considerable name value to Japanese audiences due to work in the 1960s putting him on the same level of reverence as Lou Thesz. He was respected as both a worker and a trainer, and his legacy was passed on through trainees Hiro Matsuda, Satoru Sayama, and Yoshiaki Fujiwara, who solidified Gotch's legend as 'god of wrestling'. The influence Gotch has on the medium even after his 2007 passing is felt in every German suplex, and Minoru Suzuki's trademark cradled pile driver named after the 'god'.

Bill Robinson

Japanese wrestling fans have huge respect for the British 'Lancashire' style, with its intricate submission holds and innovative counters representing as much a display of escapology as physical prowess. That deference is almost entirely due to Bill Robinson, a foreign talent only superseded in importance by Gotch himself.

The two had a history with one another before coming to Japan. Gotch, fresh off of turning pro after an amateur career that saw him compete in the Olympics, stretched a young Robinson with painful submission holds in a Wigan gym in 1954. Robinson allegedly felt bitter about that incident until the two crossed paths for IWE in April 1971, where a run of three main event draws saw them cement a partnership.

After Gotch introduced Robinson to NJPW, the Briton formed a strong relationship with Inoki that would see the Japanese Strong Style further evolve. His 1975 NWF title match with Inoki, promoted as 'free style versus Strong Style' was a thriller, and clearly demonstrated the hybrid of British and American pro wrestling styles along with the more legitimate martial arts that the Japanese style had become. On almost even footing with 'god of wrestling' Gotch as a figure of respect, Robinson was a rare foreigner that garnered a positive reaction from Japanese fans, though he was a feared trainer and opponent in a legitimate environment.

Part of the fractures in NJPW that caused the UWF and UWFi splinter groups, Robinson trained legitimate fighters as well as pro wrestlers, Kazushi Sakuraba being a notable name familiar to modern NJPW fans that studied under Robinson. For better and for worse, he was a major figure in the incorporation of shoot fighting in the Japanese style, and, indirectly the 'vale tudo' dynamic that almost sank NJPW in the early 2000s.

Dynamite Kid

Robinson and British wrestling's reach extended beyond influencing the heavyweight style in Japan. In the late 1970s and throughout the '80s, the UK's Allstar Promotions was the destination of choice for NJPW's junior heavyweight Young Lions' seasoning trips before gaining main card status. As Satoru Sayama and Keiichi Yamada both wrestled lightweight matches on Allstar's World of Sport TV show before gaining iconic gimmicks, the Anglo/Japanese door was also a two way one.

Notable moves to Japan from the UK would include Marc Rocco, an honorable mention on this list for his work as the first Black Tiger, but more influential was Tom 'Dynamite Kid' Billington. While he was perhaps most famous in Japan for his work with Davey Boy Smith as the British Bulldogs in All Japan, his feud with a re-debuting Sayama as Tiger Mask was the stuff of legend, their matches bringing a pace and athleticism unseen up to that point.

Stylistically, Billington had a huge hand in inspiring a generation of junior heavyweights, and personal demons aside, his in-ring genius cannot be denied, his influence easily felt in the work of Devitt, Benoit, and many more besides.

Tiger Jeet Singh

Gotch and Robinson were incredibly important in the early days of NJPW, their status as recognizable foreign names creating high drawing main events for Inoki. Tiger Jeet Singh though was important to the history of the company as a foreign star made within the promotion, setting the standard for the likes of Vader, and even Devitt in the future.

Canada's adopted Indian son was a limited in-ring talent, but a tremendously charismatic individual and a wonderfully fearsome character. Despised by Japanese fans ever since the angle that saw him strike Inoki's wife near a shopping centre, he was able to draw a normally reserved nation's ire. Witness a 1975 bout between Singh and Inoki, where time from ring announcement to first lock up was a huge 15 minutes thanks to an immensely hot crowd that were easily milked (literally at one point in the match's preamble, as an angry fan hurled a carton of dairy at the heel). It was all smoke and mirrors to hide a weak in-ring performance, but that's the magic of pro wrestling, and Singh was an extremely capable pro wrestler.

Singh was able to parlay this easily garnered hate into a more than two decade career in Japan, finishing with bouts into the mid 90s for Atsushi Onita's violent FMW promotion and IWA Japan, before starting a second life as a philanthropist in his adopted Canada.

AJ Styles

From January 4, 2011 to at least 2016, only three talents have held the IWGP Heavyweight championship. Hiroshi Tanahashi is the promotion's undisputed Ace. Kazuchika Okada is the young talent that management has groomed into a prospective draw for years to come. Then there's AJ Styles, one of few foreign champions in IWGP history, and inarguably the best.

Styles entered New Japan to much skepticism in 2014, and the hot-shot booking that saw him replace a leaving Devitt as Bullet Club leader and pin Okada to capture the title in the space of a month was doubted by many. Styles had toiled for years in the relatively obscure TNA, after all, a promotion that has very little coverage in Japan and meant a complete reinvention was required for Styles, a 16 year veteran at that point.

His work removed all doubt critics had. Styles' performances over the following years were the best of his long career, justifying his place in IWGP Championship history, and seeing him labelled 'the best in the world' by none other than Tanahashi himself. April 2015's Invasion Attack saw Ryogoku Sumo Hall sell out before anything was announced for the card other than Styles defending his title. Later in the year, Styles against Okada would sell out an Osaka Castle Hall the promotion hadn't dared to run in over two decades. Styles was not only a justified choice as champion, but a proven huge money maker for the company.

Chris Benoit

Every discussion of Chris Benoit, and his hard hitting style, is always overshadowed by the circumstances surrounding his murder/suicide in 2007. Separating artist from art, though, Benoit was a key contributor to NJPW in the mid 1990s as the junior heavyweight scene was flourishing.

While All Japan's heavyweights were phenomenal in the 1990s, arguably giving that promotion the edge as far as overall quality was concerned when compared to NJPW, New Japan was able to distinguish itself with a phenomenal breed of young, smaller stars. The pair of Super J Cup tournaments in 1994 for New Japan and 1995 for WAR highlighted NJPW juniors Shinjiro Otani and Koji Kanemoto, introduced to a new audience independent high fliers like Great Sasuke and Hayabusa, and drew attention to other foreigners Chris Jericho (Lionheart), Dean Malenko, and Eddie Guerrero (Black Tiger) but made a star of inaugural winner Chris Benoit.

Benoit had been in NJPW for eight years at this point, taking the rare step for foreign talent of training in the NJPW dojo and living the Japanese Young Lion lifestyle. After a brief run under his real name, Benoit was brought to the forefront as Pegasus Kid, drawing on his Calgary Canada origins, and Stu Hart training along with Dynamite Kid to present a character that was in essence a Dynamite 2.0. Benoit was a devotee of Billington's, and adopted his signature maneuvers, particularly his diving headbutt, while merging them with his own techniques to become a hugely respected star. Much as Dynamite Kid would be worshipped thanks to his battles with the original Tiger Mask, Benoit, first as Pegasus Kid and then Wild Pegasus would gain most notoriety for working with Black Tiger, portrayed at the time by Eddie Guerrero.

Paving the road for more modern stars like Devitt and Anderson of becoming an adopted and respected son of Japanese audiences by putting in the hard work in the promotion's own system, Benoit's legacy cannot and should not be ignored.

Hulk Hogan

Hulk Hogan would never reach the same level of household name fame and fortune in Japan as he would in America, but was nevertheless a huge star in his runs with NJPW in the early 1980s. This was a curious event in and of itself; Hogan was working for Vince McMahon Sr.'s WWWF at the time of his initial debut in NJPW, but after a dispute with McMahon led to him working for Verne Gagne's AWA, he would still wrestle for Inoki despite Gagne's working relationship with All Japan.

His loyalty to NJPW was possibly a result of his training under Inoki's firm friend Hiro Matsuda, and Matsuda's closeness to WWWF was a significant factor in his return to the by now more simply titled World Wrestling Federation in 1983. In the meantime, though, NJPW made Hogan into far more of a star than AWA had the resources to. Hulk was branded '*Ichiban-* Hogan' (number one), so heavily that he even had a disco album under the same name.

It was also in Japan that Hogan showed far more diversity and range as a performer than he would in his WWF heyday. Utilising a powerful Axe Bomber lariat for a finish rather than the leg drop that would destroy his hips and knees in WWF, Hogan worked a far more technical style that crowds ate up in matches against Tatsumi Fujinami and Riki Choshu. Hogan would even get the better of Inoki himself, becoming the (albeit accidental) inaugural winner of the IWGP League in the summer of 1983, making him an easy pick for this list.

Stan Hansen

As crucial as Gotch was to Japanese wrestling in the 1960s and '70s, and as worshipped he was in turn, Hansen was just as significant in the 1980s and

'90s, creating a legend that lives on to this day. Hansen was more technically gifted than Jeet Singh, but carried the same wild brawling style to the ring, unleashing flurries of punches and clubbing blows that often left opponents legitimately knocked for a loop.

Scoring a rare count out win over Inoki in his debut in 1978, Hansen was a typically hated foreign heel for the next few years, with Japanese crowds buying even more into his dangerous persona as news of his Western Lariat breaking the neck of Bruno Sammartino was relayed to them. In later work with New Japan, Hansen would inspire just as much awe, most famously in an interpromotional February 10 1990 match with Vader where an errant blow broke his opponent's orbital bone and knocked Vader's eye loose. Miraculously, Vader didn't suffer permanent damage, and the match even reached its planned double countout finish. Hansen would form a tag team with Riki Choshu named after both men's predilection for using lariats as finishers, cementing him as a loved veteran.

It was the middle years from '81 to '89 that saw Hansen have a big impact on NJPW, though. Part of an exodus of foreign talent to All Japan, Hansen was the first main player in a bidding war for foreign stars, and while Hansen would be paired with Bruiser Brody in AJPW in a team beloved by fans, the struggles he was a part of devalued foreign talent in the eyes of bookers, making successful imports in either promotion rare in years to come.

Vader

A riot would ensue in Ryogoku on Vader's debut
(Photo: Moritsuna Kimura/AFLO)

Vader was wrestling for the AWA through much of the 1980s, which would have lead to a Japanese career with Baba by default. His trainer Masa Saito, however, managed to help negotiate him over to NJPW to fill Inoki's role of a monster heel named Vader. Loosely based on folklore surrounding a real twelfth century Japanese warrior, Vader was given grand treatment, with his imposing masked costume. On December 27 1987, Vader debuted, challenging Inoki after his defeat of Riki Choshu. Vader beat Inoki in five minutes, and the Ryogoku Sumo Hall crowd rioted. While there were more factors at play, White would definitely play up his part in inciting the flaming cushion tossing crowd.

NJPW suffered a two year ban from the arena as a result, but by the time they returned, Vader had already made history as the first foreign IWGP champion, winning the title from Shinya Hashimoto in the final of a one night tournament at NJPW's first show at the new Tokyo Dome. The move demonstrated the company's faith in Vader as a leading star, and Leon White's performances as an agile big man with a vicious stiff style vindicated them.

5

Dragons, Tigers, Scorpions and Scandals

1979 saw NJPW begin a move into a new decade full of promise, unease, and downright strangeness. Inoki showed his hand as a future diplomat in January, prefacing his later relationship with North Korea by challenging Idi Amin to a match, promising to make the Ugandan leader pay for his human rights abuses. If Inoki had a hard time deciding rules for a match with a Muhammad Ali that didn't want to put the wrestler over, this was definitely ill advised, and obviously was never serious, but garnered a few headlines and furthered Inoki's image as a humanitarian fighting for the oppressed.

Later in the year, on November 30 in Tokushima, Inoki made history by defeating Bob Backlund, becoming the first (indeed, only; Samoan Rodney Anoa'i only played a Japanese national on TV as Yokozuna) Japanese holder of the recently rechristened World Wrestling Federation Heavyweight championship. Inoki would pin Backlund clean, and a melee would ensue with Tiger Jeet Singh coming to the ring and assaulting both new and former champion. A week later in Kuramae, Backlund escaped an Inoki short arm scissors by dumping the champion on the floor. Jeet Singh rushed to ringside to strike at Inoki, and as he was quickly being carted off, Backlund suplexed Inoki back into the ring and regained the WWF title. Tiger Jeet Singh's involvement in both matches would be the storyline reason for the reign being declared null and void, Backlund never having his run interrupted in the WWF's revisionist continuum.

That ongoing Inoki/Singh feud, now in its seventh year, was the basis of 1979's largest main event. A cross promotional supercard organized between NJPW, IWE and AJPW by the Tokyo Sports newspaper would see the BI Cannon reunite for one night only, facing the pairing of Singh and Abdullah the Butcher. As the Cannon triumphed, the long term rivals stood tall in front of 16,500 at the Budokan, but in truth, the inter promotional war between New and All Japan would step up considerably in the coming years.

Inoki would spend the majority of 1980 and 1981 working with Stan Hansen in a series of strong bouts, Hansen briefly winning the NWF title from Inoki via count out on February 8 1980 after hitting a lariat that sent the champion off the apron. Inoki was quick to get his clean win back less than two months later, but Hansen's character as a devious heel with the brawn to back things up was cemented in the feud. The pair wrestled several times in singles or tag matches with different partners, and on each occasion, wove their matches together in an ongoing story; Hansen often teasing hard hitting apron spots in a bid to get Inoki counted out again.

Hansen was earning the respect of Japanese crowds, but by the end of 1981, he was gone, lured away by the promise of a big money feud with Giant Baba for All Japan. A more bitter war had begun between the promotions, each company trying to outbid the other, primarily for foreign talent. Tiger Jeet Singh would also hop to All Japan in 1981, though in kind, NJPW snagged Abdullah the Butcher for his second run with the company from a top heel position with Baba, as well as Deep South star Dick Murdoch.

While other talent went to and from the company, the top foreign heavyweight spot in NJPW through the early 80's comfortably belonged to Hulk Hogan. It was a strange situation for the young Terry Bollea to be working for Inoki; Hogan had been working for the McMahons and WWF before being fired for taking the Thunderlips role in *Rocky* 3 without company say-so. He would be working for a spell with Verne Gagne in the AWA, which still had a working arrangement with Baba, but nevertheless started his Japanese career in NJPW, partly as a result of Inoki's closeness to his trainer Hiro Matsuda.

With McMahon Sr heavily involved with booking foreign talent in NJPW along with Hisashi Shinma, Hogan would have his foot wedged in the return door to WWF, and become the biggest star of the 1980s when Hulkamania began in the middle of the decade. Before that though, he had an impressive run working for and with Inoki. Tagging with Hansen in the MSG tag series tournament, he would work heel, before becoming a rare foreign babyface act in matches with Abdullah, and Andre the Giant. Hogan's still barely full head of flowing blond locks, and the muscular look that Hulkamania would be built on in WWF made him a marketable star in Japan as well. Endorsements and a Jimmy Hart penned EP named *'Ichiban'* would follow, the latter being a four track novelty disco record that, at least, didn't feature the Hulkster himself crooning, putting it a step above his later US recording effort with 'The Wrestling Boot Band'.

Hogan and Andre's Japanese meeting some time before, and some orders of magnitude beneath their famous Wrestlemania 3 match in terms of quality and interest, was part of the inaugural IWGP tournament in May 1983. NWF had long since ceased to exist as its own entity, yet the main heavyweight title in the promotion was still the NWF Heavyweight belt. As a result, Inoki started a slow process of rebranding, creating a fictional governing body for NJPW; the International Wrestling Grand Prix, or IWGP. The winner of the first tournament in '83 would be known as IWGP champion, though the championship belt as we know it today wouldn't come into effect until 1987.

Everyone, of course, expected Inoki to win the IWGP championship; he was running strong as a mainstream star, and had the luxury of booking himself to win the vast majority of his matches, or at the very least, only losing to scrappy countouts and disqualifications. It was no shock, then, when Inoki kicked out of Hogan's favoured finish at the time, the Ax Bomber lariat (a move his album would claim was actually called the Ax *Boomber*) midway through the June 3 final. It was a surprise to see Hogan land a second Ax Bomber to send Inoki flying off the apron. Inoki hit his head on the bump and was legitimately out cold. His seconds rolled him back into the ring, but Inoki remained unresponsive, and the referee stopped the match. Hogan was put over solidly, but completely by accident. As Inoki was stretchered out of the ring, melodramatic commentary ran that this was the day 'fighting spirit' died.

Inoki disappeared from NJPW tours for a few months, heading abroad in a non-wrestling capacity to back younger touring Japanese stars in other promotions including Stu Hart's Stampede Wrestling in Calgary. He would re-emerge to no small amount of controversy, but business was nonetheless strong. Through the 1980s, Asahi's World Pro Wrestling NJPW TV show had up to 26% of the audience share on TV. While Hogan could hold a small claim to drawing that audience, it was more down to a wave of strong domestic stars. They would, the hope was, not leave as easily for AJPW as the foreigners, and would be easily booked (Masa Saito, a strong advocate for NJPW to the WWF, and the man Leon White would credit for discovering and suggesting him for the Vader gimmick years later, would be out of circulation for a couple of years, jailed along with Ken Patera for throwing a rock through a McDonald's window and resisting subsequent arrest).

On the junior heavyweight front, Satoru Sayama, who was on the rise in the late 1970s, would return to Japan in April 1981 after successful tours of Mexico and the UK, where he had phenomenal matches with Jim Breaks and 'Cyanide' Sid Cooper. He returned as Tiger Mask, a character licensed from the popular early '70s manga, that TV Asahi had recently resurrected for an animated TV show. If it had some hardcore fans worried about a descent into camp that Inoki had attempted once before with kid's drama *Pro Wrestling Star Azteckaiser* (Sayama would even wrestle kid's TV hero Ultraman for a spell), fears would soon be allayed.

Sayama seemed more comfortable in this role and after international seasoning than he ever was in plain black trunks as a Young Lion. He effortlessly tied together his Strong Style strikes with high flying topes and rope feints modern WWE fans would be familiar with as Rey Mysterio's 619 move, while in the middle of the ring, thrilled with innovative offense including power bomb and suplex variants still named after him to this day. A cartoon superhero made flesh, he would beat easily cycled out foreign heels in a throwback nationalistic gimmick of sorts, including thrilling bouts with

Marc Rocco (as nemesis Black Tiger) and Tom 'Dynamite Kid' Billington before Dynamite found further fame in AJPW. Tiger Mask was a hot ticket with younger fans, and a key part of NJPW's television strategy throughout the decade; at least that was the plan.

On the heavyweight front underneath Inoki, the early 1980s belonged to Rusher Kimura, Tatsumi Fujinami and Riki Choshu.

Masao 'Rusher' Kimura had been IWE's leading star after Tokyo Pro's closure in the '60s. The former sumo wrestler turned pro had helped carve a unique niche for his promotion; New and All Japan, while given to the occasional flight of fancy and storyline driven gimmick matches, were reasonably straight laced, while IWE was a more violent promotion. Death matches were frequent, often in steel cages never adopted by their rivals, and IWE's genetics could be easily seen in later ultra violent promotions IWA Japan, W*ING (pronounced 'Wing', though cheeky native English readers could elide the 'I' and substitute another letter for the asterisk) and BJW (Big Japan Wrestling, for those with their minds still in the gutter). Despite being a strong alternative, with a keen eye for younger talent (IWE brought Andre the Giant over for his first Japanese tour), they were the third wheel in the New/All Japan rivalry, and struggling finances saw their doors closing in August 1981.

Tiger Mask and Dynamite Kid's feud were innovative displays, and drew attention to the burgeoning Junior division *Photo: Moritsuna Kimura/AFLO*

The remaining roster split into two groups, with half going to All Japan and half to New. Kimura headed up the NJPW crew, and along with Animal Hamaguchi and a selection of IWE mid carders formed the *Shin Kokusai Gundan* or New International Army.

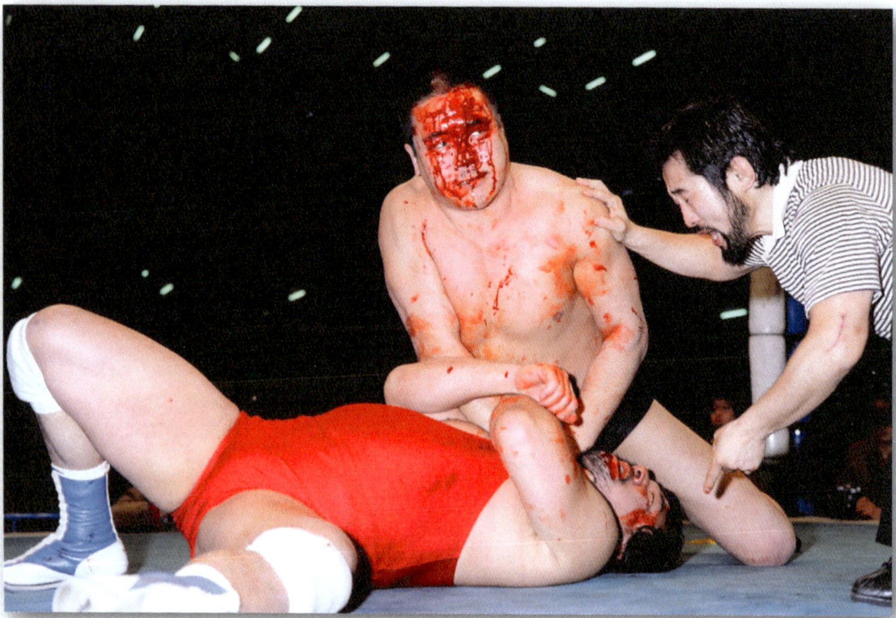

Animal Hamaguchi exemplified the bloody IWE style, here with Yoshiaki Fujiwara *Photo: Yukio Hiraku/AFLO*

Kimura hopping into the ring before an Inoki/Tiger Toguchi main event on September 23 1981, and declaring his group's presence with a simple 'good evening' was an unannounced shock. It set into motion an invasion angle of New Japan, years before the NJPW/UWFi feud that would be the pattern for the New World Order's appearance in WCW. The invasion was the backdrop for a series of Inoki/Kimura matches through '81 and '82, which included a number of gimmick matches uncharacteristic of the promotion.

Lumberjack, death and hair matches were all part of the program dubbed the Bloody Fight Series and designed to hide the fact Inoki and Kimura had little in-ring chemistry. The hair match particularly was rough, a battle of perm and pompadour that saw Inoki win but the payoff of Kimura being shorn denied the crowd. Eventually the angle lost steam in its initial incarnation, NIA stablemate Strong Kobayashi suffering a back injury which left the group wanting depth in the fan's eyes. Enter stage right, Riki Choshu, and the hottest rivalry of the '80s, with nemesis 'the dragon'.

Fujinami and Choshu's rivalry was one of the most intense in the history of the medium *Photo: Yukio Hiraku/AFLO*

Tatsumi Fujinami only grew in popularity throughout the decade, well on the way to becoming one of the most significant stars in Japanese history. Making the transition from junior to heavyweight is a risky decision that would break stars like Shinjiro Otani a decade later, but Fujinami had a smooth switch. He relinquished the WWF Junior Heavyweight championship in the autumn of 1981 at the peak of 'dragon fever' popularity, and would walk straight into a ready-made program with Choshu.

Choshu was perfectly set up to play the jealous heel against Fujinami. Rising through the heavyweight ranks in the late '70s, Choshu was poised to become the number two star behind Inoki. Yet Fujinami as a junior was getting more attention at the close of the prior decade. Fujinami would whitewash the league phase of the Pre Japan tournament, before moving to the heavyweight division and soon after winning the WWF International championship (not to be confused with the WWF/E Intercontinental championship) from Gino Brito in New York. Though as much issues of coincidence and luck as proper planning, these events could easily be seen as milestones in a five year build to the two young hopes locking horns.

This they finally did on October 8, 1982. In a six man tag featuring Inoki, Choshu and Fujinami teaming against Abdullah the Butcher, Special Delivery Jones and Bad News Allen, the youngsters clashed, tagging in with shoves and slaps to the face. After Fujinami won with a sunset flip on Allen, Choshu walked in and smacked his teammate in the head, a brawl breaking out while Inoki attempted to play peacemaker. The subtext was about Inoki, of course; the angle playing out like jealous siblings after their father's attention, but Choshu and Fujinami played their roles to the hilt. On their first meeting as opponents a month later, Fujinami came out in a distinctly Inoki like embroidered robe, an enraged Choshu attacking the International champion before the bell rang. The match was thrown out as both spilled to the outside, and while Choshu walked away as Fujinami invited his opponent to step back in, the crowd chanting for '*en-cho*' (extra time), the hook was set. Oddly though, while Choshu was painted the heel, he would earn the majority of audience chants, which spoke to the relative uniqueness at the time of two Japanese stars in a heated feud, and how much the audience had invested in both men.

Choshu would head a revitalised *Kokusai Gundan* dubbed the *Ishin Gundan*. No longer simply portrayed as a group of invaders from a collapsed IWE, the angle transformed into a story of an entirely separate company that had rebelled against NJPW brass and left.

Meanwhile the singles feud between Choshu and Fujinami escalated all through 1983, drawing huge houses, and Fujinami became the solid fan favourite, fighting on as Choshu scored a clean victory followed by a series of disqualifications and countouts. Sold out house upon sold out house would show up through 1983 and into '84, confident that this was the night The Dragon would finally be victorious, and lead the next generation of NJPW stars. They would usually be disappointed, only to buy a ticket for the next show. On July 7, Fujinami locked Choshu in his own Scorpion Deathlock finishing hold, a rare storytelling tactic at the time; but as Choshu reached the ropes, Fujinami held on and was disqualified. A mere month later, a bloodied Fujinami delivered a back drop onto the concrete floor to beat his rival, but only by count out.

Fujinami finally did get his pinfall win on July 20 1984 in Hokkaido, cementing Fujinami as a babyface on Inoki's level, while the *Ishin Gundan* was still strong. A returning Inoki got his win back over Hogan in the second IWGP tournament in '84, but Choshu and *Ishin Gundan*'s involvement after Inoki's countout victory sparked a near riot at Kuramae Sumo Hall. This spun Inoki into a singles match with Choshu, which Inoki unsurprisingly won, but interest was still phenomenally high, especially for a classic ten man tag in April that year between the NJPW team of Inoki, Fujinami, Kengo Kimura, Nobuhiko Takada and Yoshiaki Fujiwara, and the *Ishin Gundan* of Choshu, Isamu Teranishi, Kuniaki Kobayashi and the pairing of Animal Hamaguchi and Yoshiaki Yatsu, who were strong contenders in tag tournaments at the time.

In 1983, NJPW sold out 90% of their gates, and the company turned a profit of over 2.1 billion Yen, or 9 million USD, which converts to 21 million in today's money. Choshu and his group were riding high on the hottest angle in company history, and NJPW was soaring; but by the end of 1984 he and the entire *Gundan* had left for All Japan, and there were serious concerns that the house Inoki had built wouldn't survive into the second half of the decade. What happened?

Inoki's business ventures, much like mentor Rikidozan's, were not limited to pro wrestling. While Rikidozan's businesses outside of pro wrestling were somewhat clandestine, Inoki's were more clean cut in theory, including a bio-tech supplement company in his former homeland of Brazil called Anton Hisel. Even if the business was on the up-and-up, though, one thing it wasn't was successful. The company tanked, echoing WWF/E owner Vince McMahon's own experiments in supplements like IcoPro a decade later. As the ship sank, though, Inoki, with the knowledge of the rest of NJPW's top brass, continued to siphon cash from New Japan live gates into his failing secondary project.

When news reached talent at the end of '83, they were incensed. JWA had been sunk by financial mismanagement, causing Inoki to lead a coup that would see NJPW formed, and now Inoki was embezzling money from his own promotion. NJPW VP Hisashi Shinma was the sacrificial lamb fired for his involvement, losing the company a significant foreign booking voice with the NWA and WWF. Sayama, who owed a lot to Shinma's booking of him internationally and his lobbying for the Tiger Mask character, plotted his own coup; when he was found out, he left along with Rusher Kimura, Akira Maeda, Gran Hamada, Fujiwara and more. Shinma created a harder hitting martial arts oriented promotion called the Universal Wrestling Federation, or UWF (not to be confused with the Bill Watts operated US promotion of the same name), that the coup members all joined, the promotion running over the following two years.

Inoki and Seiji Sakaguchi stepped down as president and VP of New Japan temporarily, Inoki maintaining his place as main event talent. Both men would soon, mysteriously be 'voted in' to return to their positions at the top of the company. Choshu and crew were upset at the political instability, or perhaps were frustrated at the prospect of continuing to labour under Inoki's main event glass ceiling. As 1984 closed, NJPW was financially reeling, in turmoil, and with a gutted roster. They would bounce back with new titles, a more independent philosophy, and a man called Vader.

NJPW's Young Lions

There's a small, unassuming building attached to a warehouse near the banks of the Tama river in Setagaya (the second most populous of the 23 wards that make up the Tokyo metropolis), that holds a lot of history. The building, Inoki's former home, has hosted Masahiro Chono, Riki Choshu, Keiji Muto and more over five decades, as well as Jushin Liger, who incredibly has lived there for half of this time. While the WWE has a high tech performance centre, NJPW has more modest digs, dubbed the NJPW dojo.

Wrestlers are trained differently in Japan than in the west, and in a manner that highlights the origins of the medium in the country. In the US and Europe, schools would be independent, offering limited training until the fine details of performance were learned on the job. The American wrestler's existence was nomadic, and so was their training, with small schools springing up and disappearing. The idea of a feeder system, with small promotions for wrestlers to base themselves out of before making the leap to the major leagues only came up out of necessity as the erosion of old wrestling territories made that on the job training harder.

When pro wrestling took off in Japan, new talent would enter the business in a similar fashion to young sumo prospects; the medium's biggest stars early on were former sumo wrestlers, after all. Training wouldn't happen over the space of a few months, talents commuting from home to school, often being pushed to their breaking points in a bid to see whether they had the mettle to drive back the next day. It wasn't a 9-5 proposition, or something done by prospects after a day job. It would be a 24/7 experience, and over a much longer period.

As such, prospects would sleep in a building attached to the dojo, and more than simply training a few hours a day, would also cook and clean for established talents, over and above up to eleven hours of practice, mirroring the lifestyle at a sumo stable. A trainee allowed to commute in to practice was rare, and often the recipient of some resentment, as was the case when Shohei Baba was allowed to live in an apartment near the JWA dojo as he trained. Hiroshi Tanahashi would live in the NJPW dojo for four years; Liger never left.

In keeping with the NJPW lion mark theme, the company's young stars were quickly labelled 'Young Lions', among their first being Tatsumi Fujinami, a student of Inoki during the JWA days, and an opening act in NJPW's early years aged just 16. The Young Lion pattern from first training to main card status was the same in the mid '70s as it would be in the mid 2010s for the most part; prospects train, before working preliminary matches for a certain period, and then make a foreign excursion, returning with a character to portray on TV.

Even entering the dojo is a tall order; much like WWE's system in the States, there are stringent requirements to meet and a demanding physical tryout to clear. It's an initial hurdle many tumble at; Yoshi-Hashi failed the initial test twice before entering the dojo after a student dropped out. Tetsuya Naito in a 2015 interview recalled enrolling in the same tryout as Kazuchika Okada, who struggled through the tryout despite his prior training under Ultimo Dragon in the Toryumon promotion.

Training itself is demanding to the point of danger; Hiromitsu Gompei's death during training in 1995 being shrouded in secrecy, but allegedly being due to Kensuke Sasaki pressing the young charge too hard. Extremely rigorous training, and a system of coaches verbally berating and physically assaulting trainees is commonplace in Japanese sports, and striking youngsters with kendo sticks when errors are made is not a practice limited to Satoru Sayama's infamous MMA training.

The Yomiuri Giants baseball team's legendarily harsh training lead to the 1973 suicide of Toshihiko Yoguchi, and as in the corporate world, *karoshi* (death from overwork) has been a very real problem in sports. There has been a gradual change in this regard, and a move to a more positive training regimen has begun of late. That's arguably been led again by sumo, albeit as a result of negative press; in 2007 a sumo stable master called Tokitsukaze earned front page headlines and a five year jail term after he ordered his trainees to regularly beat 17 year old Tokitaizan with canes and other weapons; the youngster died as a result. Today's dojo is strenuous, but not lethally so.

Once accepted into the dojo, prospects live in one of the seven attached rooms, only allowed to leave if they drop out of the system, or make their main roster debut. They train, as well as maintain the dojo for any talent that stops by to use it. They cook *chanko* (a protein rich stew that's traditional fare for sumo wrestlers), for everyone, clean, and essentially have their lives focussed on wrestling for 24 hours a day. When there's a New Japan show, it's the Young Lions that set up and take down the ring, performing roadie like work as needed; once trainees have some time under their belts, they're able to watch matches from ringside, newcomers have to earn that honour.

One of the bigger changes in the current NJPW product as opposed to the promotion's beginnings is in the presentation of debuting young stars. The philosophy is the same; as a rule Young Lions are perennial 'jobbers', working often with one another and occasionally with a main roster talent in a losing tag team effort. In the past however, youngsters were perhaps given more opportunities to shine, first through the Karl Gotch Cup between 1974 and '76, which had Tatsumi Fujinami as its inaugural winner, then to the Young Lions Cup which had a similarly short run in the 1980s. It would be a launching pad for a young star, with the winner usually making his foreign excursion shortly afterward and returning with a big win under their belt and an established jumping off point.

Today though, without a dedicated tournament for debuting talent, or initiatives like the U-30 Championship the company briefly dabbled with in the mid 2000s, Young Lions often seem somewhat aimless in their roles, the key 'flipping of the switch' being when they earn a character.

Black tights and black boots were *de rigeur* for the early years of wrestling, and, certainly in NJPW, it wasn't until Tiger Mask and the like that more extravagant ring gear and a 'gimmick' so to speak became part of a Japanese star's character. Today, with the exception of throwbacks like Katsuyori Shibata, everyone has a gimmick, but that's a right to be earned. Freshly debuting Young Lions working opening matches have black tights, black boots, and rarely even knee or elbow pads. To go along with that, they have to work in a limited style, and aren't allowed to showcase particular signature moves or holds until much later. Instead a Young Lion match will always end in the same way, with a submission finish from a Boston Crab or variant thereof. It can result in some dry opening bouts for fans, but also lets the true potential of a wrestler shine; it's genuinely interesting to see a young star work within very strict confines, but still win a crowd over and seem memorable. To a hardcore audience, following a Young Lion and gradually seeing them progress, earning a kneepad here, or a new move there, is extremely gratifying, and it's the familiarity, and sense of loyalty that audiences have with a character that makes them more enduring as main event stars. From Fujinami and Choshu, through Chono, Shinya Hashimoto, Satoshi Kojima and Shinjiro Otani, up to (hopefully) today's Sho Tanaka and Yohei Komatsu; fan love runs a long way back, and very deep.

Aware, though, that staying and learning in one dojo with a limited group of opponents in front of similar audiences can lead to homogeneity, the tradition from Rikidozan all the way up to current stars has been to send prospects abroad. Heading to Mexico, Europe and the US, wrestlers undergo a period of learning and growth before returning with a full fledged character. Some of these trips are extremely successful, making wrestlers like Keiji Muto world renowned, as he developed the Great Muta gimmick. Others, like Okada given an embarrassing Green Lantern themed gimmick of Okato in TNA, might be experiences the talent in question would rather fans forget, but they invariably make wrestlers more well rounded, not just as a wrestler, but as a human being.

'Everyone has to make these trips before they debut, so they know what it's like to be in a strange locker room, perhaps not speaking the language,' former IWGP Junior Heavyweight champion Rocky Romero explains. 'It means the atmosphere (for a foreign talent) in the locker room is much more relaxed. There's always Liger, or (Yuji) Nagata, coming up to you, relaxing, making jokes. It's a cool atmosphere'.

Returning more worldly wise, and more experienced, wrestlers are then left to sink or swim in the main card mix. It's a demanding route from newcomer to NJPW star, but the Young Lion lifestyle is a proven one, and one more holistic than at first appears; turning out not just experienced wrestlers, but more complete human beings as they grow up within the system.

6

Predicting A Riot

The Anton Hisel scandal was a wave that rippled outward over the course of the next five years or so. It would have at least an indirect hand in a series of blows to New Japan that would have sunk a company in a weaker state, or in a weaker economy, the rising tide of Japan's bubble helping to raise all ships.

On Halloween 1985, the WWF cut ties with NJPW, resulting in the WWF Junior Heavyweight title being retired along with the International Tag Team championship, which was stripped from the team of Tatsumi Fujinami and Kengo Kimura. This wasn't entirely a result of the furore surrounding Inoki; Vince McMahon Jr had by this point taken over company reigns from his late father. With a different, more aggressive business philosophy, the younger McMahon wasn't as interested in booking talent to or from Japan as his father was, instead concentrating on massive national expansion and the erosion of the territorial system in the States.

Still, there was no doubt that the tribulations of '83 had a hand in things falling apart. With Hisashi Shinma being the fall guy to be fired from the scandal, a crucial tie to the WWF had been lost, and it didn't help that Masa Saito was in jail for the McDonald's incident at this point, too.

A couple of years later, the NWA and NJPW parted ways as well. The days of the American wrestling scene being a cabal of promoters that locked talent up were largely gone, allowing NJPW to negotiate with a lot of foreign talent directly, but this was still a convenient working relationship lost. Easy access to big name foreigners was harder now, and with the hit of Satoru Sayama and Riki Choshu's crews both leaving, times were tough.

To compound things, a negative air hung around Inoki himself. In May 1986, tabloid magazine *Friday* exposed Inoki for cheating on his wife, an incident that saw Inoki publicly shave his head (shaving of the head is a common act of contrition in Japan with embattled celebrities often shedding hair to apologize for drug and sex scandals). There was a slight feeling of unease around NJPW and wrestling in general, and with sagging ratings, TV Asahi would make the call in 1988 to take the weekly World Pro Wrestling show away from prime time and onto a tougher Saturday afternoon time slot. The time of 26% rating shares wouldn't come back.

Yet for all of the outside issues that affected the company, the in-ring product had never been better. With the WWF and NWA on the way out, the fictional IWGP was phased in completely as a governing body, and new titles were created. This meant that for the first time since the company's formation, NJPW felt like its own completely independent entity. In December '85, Fujinami and Kimura made the transition from WWF International to IWGP Tag champions, the first titles under the governing body's 'purview'. A bigger surprise was how the belts were won. In the finals of a tournament, the combo beat Inoki and Seiji Sakaguchi when Fujinami pinned Inoki, clean, with a Dragon Suplex. Inoki doing the honours was a rarity; to a fellow Japanese even rarer, and with an undisputed finish practically unheard of.

Fujinami, thanks in no small part to the program with Choshu, had by this point arrived. A more mature and rounded talent now in his early thirties, Fujinami tagged and wrestled sporadically in the mid '80s with Junji Hirata, who portrayed a masked giant named Super Strong Machine (the program would also feature the appearance of a masked Andre the Giant as Super Strong's rival Giant Machine, which was slightly goofy; Andre would also team with 'Super Machine' Bill Eadie during this time, before Eadie would gain more fame as half of WWF tag team Demolition). He would transition from here into a significant program with Akira Maeda, which was a big draw for audiences in 1986.

Maeda was a friend of Satoru Sayama's, the former Tiger Mask scouting him in 1977. Like Sayama, Maeda followed the pattern of wrestling as a Young Lion in NJPW before working for a spell in the UK, where he became known for his variety of suplexes. When the Anton Hisel controversy hit, Maeda was part of Sayama's attempted coup, and subsequently was part of the group leaving to start the UWF.

Shinma and Sayama's promotion was an absolute failure, lasting barely a year. Differences over philosophy were partly to blame; in a bid to distinguish itself, the UWF adopted a 'shoot style' philosophy that was somewhat in line with Inoki's passion for mixed martial arts. It was a good deal more hard hitting than regular NJPW fare however, which led to more traditional workers like Rusher Kimura moving to AJPW.

Meanwhile Maeda and Sayama had a falling out over the company's direction going forward, leading to worked matches degenerating into legitimate fights as the friendship dissolved. Maeda was fired and an incensed Sayama left into semi retirement; without meaningful leadership the company folded.

Maeda subsequently returned with the majority of the UWF roster to New Japan at the end of 1985, in a move dubbed the 'UWF U-turn'. NJPW were able to build on what they had achieved with the *Ishin Gundam* angle and run yet another invasion angle through 1986; these successes having a large part to do with the emphasis on stables that runs through most Japanese wrestling promotions today. In this case there was a twist; unlike with the IWE members joining NJPW a few years later, there was legitimate distrust of the UWF returnees from the Inoki loyalists like Fujinami, and there was the added layer of a clash in philosophy. The medium was at a crossroads in Japan; should the country at large follow American wrestling in emphasizing glitz and glamour, or maintain an earnest and hard-hitting sports style philosophy?

From an in-ring product standpoint, the clash in styles lead to exciting bouts that drew hot crowds intrigued by the blurring of lines between fiction and reality; in many ways, the UWF U turn achieved what Inoki wanted to pull off with the Real Martial Arts title far more effectively. These were mainly people who had been trained and wrestling in NJPW's own system before leaving and returning with a harder shoot style edge; a far smoother proposition when it came to TV and live presentation than attempting to have legitimate sportsmen from other domains participate in worked matches.

It was an angle that burned brightly and evaporated quickly. The legitimate heat and stiffer UWF style lead to a lot of shots being laid in; a Fujinami and Maeda match from the summer of '86 saw the Dragon's face all but explode off of Maeda's heel, and a heated match that was building well crash to a halt. Maeda continued to prove dangerous to work with, eventually leading to his dismissal.

The NJPW vs UWF bouts, including a recreation of the ten man *Ishin*/NJPW elimination match with Maeda, Yoshiaki Fujiwara, Osamu Kido, Nobuhiko Takada and Kazuo Yamazaki forming the UWF team against an NJPW side where Inoki relinquished his captaincy to the younger Fujinami, saw if nothing else Fujinami becoming a made man. Inoki may well have been the perennial ace, but Fujinami was 1A, and with his main eventer status confirmed in the mid '80s after becoming inaugural IWGP Tag champion with Kimura, some good had come from the WWF split.

As WWF International became IWGP Tag Champions, the WWF Junior Heavyweight title, which had almost exclusively been a tool to establish the lighter division in NJPW, became the IWGP Junior Heavyweight championship. In the 1990s, where New Japan was competing with an inarguably stronger product from AJPW on the heavyweight side of things, it would be the juniors that the company would be all but built around, and the latter half of the '80s saw the formation of that.

In the new Ryogoku sumo hall on February 6 1986, Shiro Koshinaka (a former student of Giant Baba's, Koshinaka had been lured to NJPW after a perceived shunning from an AJPW that pushed Mitsuharu Misawa as its ace instead), won a tournament to become the inaugural IWGP Junior Heavyweight champion. As the belt changed hands between Koshinaka, Nobuhiko Takada, Kuniaki Kobayashi, Hiroshi Hase, and Owen Hart before landing on Jushin Liger at the end of the decade, only one of the belt's early holders, Kobayashi, was over the age of 30 when winning the title.

The IWGP Junior title matches weren't just a chance to showcase a different, more high flying style of wrestling, but also a chance to showcase younger talents, and indeed draw in younger fans. In the early '80s, kids flocked to see Sayama embody Tiger Mask, a real life superhero before their very eyes. With memories of the early '80s anime fading, and the rights to the character sold away, an opportunity was sought to repeat the real life comic book star pattern. A rookie Keiji Muto placed under the science fiction Space Lone Wolf character never caught on in '86, lacking cartoons or comic books based on him, and being more than a little too twee for shows being headlined by Maeda and Fujinami.

TV Asahi's 1989 anime *Jushin Liger* though, was part of a new wave of Japanese animation that was drawing in kids and teens that would be easily convinced to sit at the TV for World Pro Wrestling's new Saturday afternoon time slot. Keichi Yamada filled the role, and after a shaky debut with an entrance and costume that was slightly too high camp, he would set about defining the Junior Heavyweight division in the 1990s, becoming a heavy influence for a generation of stars at home and abroad.

Among the early stars of the rechristened IWGP Junior division were a pair of Canadians in Owen Hart and Chris Benoit, who wrestled as Pegasus Kid and had trained with Owen's father, Stu. They were two of a new generation of foreign stars in the post WWF/NWA era, wherein NJPW was a destination and a proving ground for younger wrestlers. Talent targeted and aspired to be a part of New Japan on their own terms rather than being sent over by their respective offices in the Americas or Europe. Once tied to a specific Japanese company by their bookings back home, and the allegiances their promoters had formed, wrestlers were able to pick their spots more easily since the pilfering of the likes of Hansen and Dynamite Kid by AJPW in the early '80s; it was a less convenient system than the old working relationships from a promoter's standpoint, but better for individual talents.

Dick Murdoch was an AJPW star who moved the opposite direction to Dynamite, and so was Bruiser Brody. Brody and Stan Hansen had brought the tag team act that had served them well in the American territories to All Japan, and crowds for Baba ate it up. Both were wild brawlers, but Brody was a leaner and more athletic ying to Hansen's stocky and brutish yang, and adored by the All Japan audience. With the prospect of more money working for Inoki playing on his mind though, Brody made the jump in March of 1985 straight into a main event program with the NJPW president, the highlight of which being an electric one hour draw in Osaka on September 16 1986.

Brody and Inoki worked brilliantly together, and it's a shame their feud was cut short *Photo: Yukio Hiraku/AFLO*

Brody and Inoki never saw eye to eye though, and disagreements as Brody attempted to engineer a working relationship with World Class in the States as well as squabbles over finishes (the Inoki and Sakaguchi glass ceilings being firmly back in place after their reinstatement in power) meant for a bumpy road. Brody, along with Jimmy Snuka, with whom he had been sporadically teaming, walked out of the 1986 Japan Cup Tag League and would never come back; if there were ever potential for fences to be mended, it would be dashed by Brody's murder in a Puerto Rico locker room in 1988.

Brody wasn't to be the long term top foreign draw he could have been for Inoki, but as the NJPW/UWF feud played out and Japanese stars drew strong houses on their own, Inoki still had a vision for a character played by a big foreign star. Big Van Vader, the plan was, would be a character based on the warrior Vader of Japanese legend, but with a science fiction twist; appealing to the young anime and manga obsessed teens while hopefully being less campy than the doomed Space Lone Wolf. Inoki envisaged an imposing figure with an ornate head set, an almost steampunk version of ancient samurai armour with jets that would spew steam and an in-built mic to address the crowd in booming voice.

The character was on the drawing board for quite some time with no-one to fill it; Masa Saito had been recommending a huge Californian by the name of Leon White to Inoki, after he was impressed by his appearances on German tours. Saito would then be incarcerated, and on his release, couldn't get hold of the big man. Inoki was close to bringing in a young and inexperienced but physically impressive Jim Hellwig for the role, but Hellwig would sign with the WWF, becoming the Ultimate Warrior. Eventually Saito and White's paths did manage to cross, and he would be brought in toward the end of a hectic and controversial 1987.

Much of the controversy came from an unlikely source. Kitano 'Beat' Takeshi was inescapable on Japanese TV at the time. Gaining infamy for being half of a low-brow mean spirited comedy double act in the late '70s, Takeshi transitioned into hosting prime time TV game shows, most famously *Takeshi no Jo* (Takeshi's Castle) which was a huge ratings draw at the time. Soon to make his directorial debut, Takeshi was a major celebrity and quickly found his face plastered over all manner of events and products.

He would be the first Japanese celebrity to have a licensed video game based upon him, despite publicly stating his distaste for the medium; the resulting *Takeshi no Chosen* (Takeshi's Challenge), which he had a hand in development of, is widely regarded as one of the worst games of all time. Takeshi was, however, a big wrestling fan, and Inoki practically jumped at the chance to bring the TV star to NJPW.

Takeshi would head up a stable of wrestlers called the TPG - Takeshi *Puroresu Gundan* or 'Takeshi's wrestling army'. He would be a heelish hype man, berating the NJPW stars for growing too soft, as fans unwilling to see a non wrestler heavily involved with NJPW TV booed him out of the building.

The angle was pushed hard though; Takeshi had Masa Saito as his muscle, Saito having worked a series of main events with Inoki over the summer, which included a bizarre and bloody no-rope handcuff match and (naturally) a defeat at the hands of the ace when Inoki became the inaugural IWGP Heavyweight Champion in June.

Later that October, Inoki and Saito would duke it out on the small island of Ganryujima, between the mainland Honshu and southern Kyushu. The match took the empty arena atmosphere devoid of fans to the logical extreme of having absolutely nothing in the area surrounding the ring but grass. One of wrestling's most bizarre, and frankly boring bouts of all time, Inoki ended up winning by putting a bloodied Saito to sleep in the same way any viewing audience would have been long before. Bizarrely, NJPW would return to this same format in 1991 as a Hiroshi Hase turning heavyweight would take on Tiger Jeet Singh in a similarly odd, emotionless affair, although one with slightly more action.

In storyline, Saito would steadily recruit a young generation of stars, many of whom had previously been feuding with a stable of Inoki's old guard that would destroy NJPW's current crop. They would include a returning Riki Choshu, lured back over from AJPW, and later (significantly for modern fans) the tag team of Crush and Punish, more well known today as Jado and Gedo.

The ringer of the group, though, would be Big Van Vader, whose arrival was hyped for weeks by Saito and the loudmouth comic. On the last show of 1987 on December 27, Vader arrived in a notorious debut that walked the line between success and disaster.

Despite being a heel character on NJPW TV, Takeshi was getting what wrestling pundits often call 'the wrong kind of heat'. He was riling fans up, but more inspiring them to change the channel rather than buy a ticket. To purists, he was making a mockery of the medium, and even casual fans were somewhat aware that this brash personality wasn't a wrestler and therefore would unlikely get what he had coming to him. The angle was more akin to the obsession with mainstream celebrity involvement commonplace in America, not in Japan, and fans of the idea were few.

Choshu would effectively pick up where he left off with Fujinami on his return. *Photo: Yukio Hiraku/AFLO*

On this winter night in 1987, the Ryogoku crowd was especially hostile toward Takeshi's antics; it was a rowdy house of revellers that were likely taking in a wrestling show as part of business or social *bonenkai*, (lit. 'forget the year party', a gathering with co-workers or circles of friends where the objective is to get so blindingly drunk that the trials of the previous year are forgotten and one can start afresh in January). They were already heckling and hurling rubbish at the ring, when it was teased that the main event of Inoki and Vader would be denied them, replaced by the tag team of Fujinami and Kimura taking on Saito and Choshu.

The traditional streamers thrown into the ring to celebrate the entrance or victory of a hero were replaced by streams of toilet paper tossed at Choshu as he clobbered Kimura with a lariat to win. While generating such raw emotion from the crowd is usually a good thing, there was a feeling that the talent had lost control, that audience protest was more about the booking than the in-ring work. Inoki headed to the ring and beat Choshu afterward, before calling out Saito and Vader to wrestle after all.

Vader removed his slightly goofy head dress and proceeded to dominate Inoki, destroying him in short order with a powerslam. Inoki, of course, had an 'out'; he had just wrestled Choshu after all, but the company president had never been destroyed so convincingly. Strangely, the baying crowd were stunned into silence, almost disbelieving. Announcers, short on time and perhaps sensing that things could grow ugly, hurriedly wished the audience a happy holiday season and signed off. Then, things indeed grew hostile.

A drunk crowd, angry at being baited and switched, and more enraged at the angle heavy five minute main event than by Inoki's upset loss, hurled whatever they found into the ring, as White quickly made a beeline for a waiting car. Some fans picked up the loose cushions that are used for seating at sumo halls and set fire to them before tossing them.

Embarrassed, and with a livid venue and TV Asahi to deal with, NJPW were banned from Ryogoku for two years, and heavily diminished Takeshi's role in the promotion. Still, there was something in the hot crowd that let the company know that the more youthful stable of TPG could make money.

Inoki, to his own credit, alongside Seiji Sakugchi in the booking role, made efforts to establish a new generation to lead NJPW into the 1990s. Inoki had high profile matches establishing both Vader and Bam Bam

Bigelow, who passed through Japan in between stints with the WWF, and was an athletic big man that proved a decent foil for Leon White.

Rumours began to circulate as to how much longer Inoki would remain an in-ring competitor, as he seemed to take a diminished role; indeed Inoki would only ever be a one time IWGP champion. After a fractured left foot led him to vacate the belt, Fujinami upset Vader to become the second IWGP champion, sparking a feud with the intimidating American that lasted for the rest of 1988. Inoki returned that August to challenge for the title he never lost, and as the match (rumoured, but never officially announced as a retirement match) ended in a one hour draw, Inoki gave Fujinami the seal of approval, shaking hands with the Dragon and Choshu, who was watching at ringside. A tearful Inoki left the ring, the torch having been passed, and would spend the next few months 'starting over' and working opening matches.

Underneath Fujinami, Saito and Choshu there was a brace of young talent in the mid card mix, mirroring the youth movement in the junior division. The Young Lion Cup had been established in 1985 as a showcase for recent dojo graduates. While its inaugural winner, Shoji Kosugi, would have an unremarkable career, and retire shortly afterward due to back problems, the 1986 winner Keichi Yamada would, as we've seen, soon transform into Jushin Liger, and the '87 champion would achieve even more.

The American born Masahiro Chono, along with Shinya Hashimoto, whom he defeated in the Young Lion Cup finals, and Keiji Muto, who had managed to recover from the Space Lone Wolf gimmick to be a sometime tag partner of Inoki during the TPG feud, would come to be known as the *Tokon Sanjushi* ('Three Musketeers of the fighting spirit'). All three would spend the latter part of the decade abroad, in Puerto Rico (in Chono and Hashimoto's case) and most notably for Muto, the NWA territories as the Alliance transitioned into WCW.

In America, Muto was rebranded as The Great Muta, a mysterious demonic creature spewing poisonous green mist into his opponent's faces in a homage to The Great Kabuki, who had made waves through the NWA and World Class promotions in the early '80s in between stints for All Japan. It was a huge transformation from the baby faced earnest youngster to demonic alter ego, and when he returned to New Japan, his ability to transform into the different personae made him a compelling character.

Muto wouldn't return until 1990, but with Chono and Hashimoto coming back to Japan toward the end of 1988, both were around for NJPW's largest show to date. Japan's biggest baseball team, the Yomiuri Giants, had just had a new home constructed for them, moving from Suidobashi's Korakuen Stadium down the road to the Tokyo Dome. NJPW presented the first wrestling show from the new venue, dubbed Super Powers Clash, on April 24, 1989.

With IWGP champion Fujinami injured with a herniated disc, the title had been vacated, leading to a one night tournament. Chono and Hashimoto both participated, Chono falling to Vader in the first round, while Hashimoto surprisingly reached the finals. He would upset Choshu in under five minutes, cradling the tournament favourite as he attempted to put on the Scorpion Death Lock before again falling to new champion Vader. There was a unique aura around Hashimoto, even early in his career; a stocky individual, he presented a different look to the leaner muscled stars like Fujinami, Inoki or fellow rookie Chono. It was a look that made his athletic spin kicks look more solid, as well as his 'Deadly Drop' DDT variant, and made him a fine opponent for the similarly agile giant Vader.

The tournament was the highlight of a middling show, which also featured Liger's debut against Kuniaki Kobayashi, and a series of Russian amateur wrestling and judo stars sprinkled through the card, and in the main event, Inoki's return to show closing status in a no ropes martial arts match with Shota Chochishvili. The Russian influence was political in nature; Inoki was now eager to start a career in the Japanese Diet (similar to the US' House of Congress) after forming the Sports Peace Party. Russian sports stars were brought to NJPW, and in return, Inoki staged the USSR's first pro-wrestling card, in a bid to strengthen relations with the Soviet nation shortly before the collapse of the Berlin Wall.

Japan versus Russia was a theme through Super Powers Clash, highlighting Inoki's political aspirations. *Photo: Moritsuna Kimura/AFLO*

It was also, for better or for worse, a chance for Inoki to reinvigorate his Real Martial Arts belt, which had largely been forgotten about since the late '70s, and only briefly brought back as a vanity item from time to time (on Inoki's 25th career anniversary in June '86, Inoki would defeat Leon Spinks by pinfall, in an even duller boxer vs wrestler match than the Ali fight; at least Spinks was willing to do the honours). There was at least some feeling that this was a reactionary move on Inoki's part, taking aim at competition that was rapidly gaining momentum. NJPW drew a more than respectable 43,800 paying fans for Super Powers Clash, but would be outdrawn in the same venue mere months later by competition from a familiar, yet surprising, source.

The King's Estates: NJPW's Vital Venues

With Japan being such a physically smaller market than the United States, NJPW is afforded more personality as a national promotion than touring American companies. As weekly US wrestling can often feel homogenous and lacking in local flavour (at least visually as sets and production rarely change), NJPW and other Japanese companies adapt to the venues and markets they're in, not just working differently to appeal to audience tastes, but also highlighting how visually different buildings are as opposed to the typical Western sports arena.

NJPW tours across the whole country; as far north as Sapporo on the frigid island of Hokkaido, and as far south as the tropical archipelago of Okinawa. International touring, often with partner promotions like Ring of Honor Stateside and Revolution Pro in the UK, has seen New Japan stars given the chance to work in front of Western fans increasingly familiar with the Japanese style and appreciative of talent making the trip. On their own, NJPW has also made advances in the rest of South East Asia, with Taiwan and Singapore becoming key expanding markets.

All that said, however, NJPW's fans are most numerous, and most vocal in the nation's capital of Tokyo and its third most populous city of Osaka. The history of the company seeps in through the walls of the venues they run, and in this chapter, we're going to take a look at the five most important venues in the hearts and minds of the New Japan fan.

Ota City Gymnasium

Located in the Ota-ku section of Tokyo, The city gymnasium is right on the outskirts of the metropolis, a stone's throw from the blue collar industrial town of Kawasaki, and a short train ride from Inoki's birthplace of Yokohama.

A small municipal gym, it's a venue most commonly used for hosting basketball matches, as well as the occasional boxing bout and volleyball tournament; to NJPW it's most significant for hosting the debut New Japan show. A short show that highlighted a lack of early roster depth in the company, it offered six international matches, with the story of the night being Japanese undercard talent (a teenage Tatsumi Fujinami and solid if uncharismatic Osamu Kido) being defeated in their matches before Rikidozan devotee Shoji Kai turned the tide, and Kotetsu Yamamoto tied things up for the Japanese by defeating the Durango brothers. It all lead to proud president Inoki taking on Karl Gotch, and losing in a typical show of humility for a debuting talent (Inoki would more than right his win-loss record later).

Lately, it's been a place New Japan runs annually on or around March 6th to commemorate another year in business. With basketball not being a particularly popular sport in Japan, it's a small venue, and wrestling shows have a slightly empty feel as spectators gather on the few bleacher seats. It's acoustically strong though, and fans that do show up to the anniversary shows usually make a lot of noise. The anniversary typically falls on a weeknight, making it the most hardcore of fans attending the events; it shows.

Korakuen Hall

Opening in April 1962, Korakuen Hall was a key part of Tokyo's Olympic bid for 1964. The Olympics, heralded as an indicator of Japan's restoration and recovery from the war two decades prior, would have most events in the westward end of the city, with the Suidobashi area and Tokyo station itself largely untouched. Boxing was the main exception, with Korakuen Hall playing host to those events.

Today, the hall is part of the larger Tokyo Dome City, with the huge Dome itself surrounded by restaurants, a shopping mall and an amusement park. In the '60s, none of this was present; the Tokyo (now Yomiuri) Giants playing baseball in Korakuen Stadium further down the road. Korakuen Hall's boxing, and subsequently wrestling events were a focal part of the Suidobashi area as it became more built up over the second half of the twentieth century. To that end, it's no surprise that Suidobashi would become the wrestling capital of Japan, or that the streets immediately surrounding its station would become home to a huge array of shops, both large and hole-in-the-wall, selling official NJPW merchandise, or a variety of combat sports knick-knacks and collectibles.

Today, many of the wrestling shops near Korakuen Hall are gone (though some remain, along with Toru Yano's bar Ebrietas, which is a common post show hang out for wrestlers having just worked the nearby venues) but the hall itself radiates history. Its relatively cheap rental price makes it an attractive venue for promotions large and small, and combat sports events take place on at least a weekly basis there.

Walk up the stairs to the hall itself, and you're treated to a veritable memory lane, as decades of show attendees queueing on the steps have whiled away the time by scrawling on the walls, often with dates and main events they had paid to see. Hansen, Inoki, Gotch, all the way to Nagata, Tanahashi, Nakamura; all are names on display, as the walls themselves seem to talk.

There's a reverence for Korakuen from anyone who wrestles there, and a reverence from the fans themselves; to that end, very often the (intimate, with a 2005 capacity) Korakuen audience can be the most critical and passionate anywhere in the country or the world. Often home to a contrary crowd, in recent years it's been a venue that beloved ace Hiroshi Tanahashi is booed in, while young stars are cheered. A Tanahashi/Prince Devitt New Japan Cup meeting in 2013 was the perfect fit for Devitt's transition to the heavyweight ranks, as fans cheered the upstart Irishman, and Tanahashi was the perfect foil, adapting and working heel; all seeds planted for Devitt to form the Bullet Club mere months later. When he returned to the same building that summer for the Best of the Super Junior finals, he defeated Alex Shelley with the supposedly cynical and world wise 21st century audience nearly incensed into a riot.

In these days of NJPW more comfortably able to draw bigger houses than in darker times, Korakuen Hall has played host to smaller shows designed to build up to major events at Ryogoku, Osaka Prefectural and the like. All the same, it's the venue that talents seem to work slightly harder at, and where the fans seem to be orders of magnitude more raucous.

Tokyo Dome

A stone's throw from Korakuen Hall is the current home of the Yomiuri Giants, and site of NJPW's biggest show of the year, the Tokyo Dome. Starting construction in 1985, and opening in 1988, the 'Big Egg', as the building is sometimes known for its shape and shell-like roof, was the ultimate symbol for the hubristic bubble economy in the Japanese '80s. Baseball matches were its primary use, but the Dome would also become a popular concert venue, and Inoki and company were keen to bring their biggest shows to the biggest venue in the country with its potential for 70,000 paying customers.

Prior to the Dome's construction, the Nippon Budokan was NJPW's venue of choice for major events; it was the site of Inoki/Ali for one. The Budokan would quickly be abandoned by NJPW after the Dome was complete, and would later host major shows for AJPW and NOAH. While NJPW's competitors would also run the Dome periodically, it would become synonymous with New Japan among wrestling fans, attendance there being a reliable metric for company fortunes.

April 24 1989 would see the first NJPW show at the Dome, and wrestling's first stadium show in more than two decades. It drew a strong 43,800 odd fans to a show that ended with Inoki being knocked out in the fifth round of his no-ropes match for the Martial Arts title, a match that highlighted Inoki's obsession with MMA on the biggest stage NJPW had ever seen. It was a long show at 14 matches, but a decent card overall. The best (and worst) would be yet to come at the Dome.

On February 10 1990, NJPW drew 53,900 to see Superfight, a card built around NJPW and AJPW stars competing in cross promotional matches for the first time since the Tokyo Sports organised card in '79. While the biggest interpromotional matches of Genichiro Tenryu and Mitsuharu Misawa (as Tiger Mask) taking on Riki Choshu and George Takano, and Stan Hansen against Vader ended in a countout and a non finish respectively (the latter seeing Hansen infamously knock Vader's eye out), it was a popular show with fans. Incredibly, wrestling was such a strong draw that a still respectable 43,700 flocked to the Dome just two months later, this time for a WWF, AJPW and NJPW joint show headlined by Hulk Hogan beating Stan Hansen.

1992 saw New Japan start an annual tradition of hosting their biggest show on January 4 at the Dome, and drew well consistently through the decade at the building before peaking in 1998. On April 4, the company had its biggest crowd in history of 57,000 (inflated to 60,000 by the company) to see Inoki beat Don Frye in his last official match.

The company drew well up to the early 2000s, but from here the freefall of bad decisions and the economic bubble well and truly popping saw houses shrink. Running too often at an expensive venue, the company drew a paltry 16,000 with Brock Lesnar in the main event in October 2005, and from here cooler heads prevailing at owners Yuke's and then Bushiroad would see the company only running the Dome for Wrestle Kingdom in January. Still, the company drew fewer than 20,000 for the next few years, before finally picking up. 36,500 paid attendees at Wrestle Kingdom 9 is some way off the 1990s heyday, but with no complimentary tickets, and a configuration that showed off huge production values with a giant stage eating space, NJPW is finally able to silence critics that once felt the Dome should be abandoned altogether.

Ryogoku Sumo Hall

Kokugikan sumo halls have been the host for pro wrestling in Japan since the medium's inception, partly due to the cross-over between the two fields. Ryogoku replaced Kuramae as Tokyo's most significant sumo hall in 1985, and NJPW also made the transition. The prior sumo hall had seen significant JWA cards, the debut of Tiger Jeet SIngh, the inaugural IWGP tournament, and a good deal of Riki Choshu and Tatsumi Fujinami's huge feud. Hosting a larger, but similarly passionate crowd to Korakuen of up to 11,066, Ryogoku would see the tradition of big matches and hot crowds continue. Almost literally in fact, as fans peppered the ring with burning cushions when Vader debuted in 1987 during a riot as the new foreigner defeated Inoki.

The company would return in 1989, and run shows consistently through the coming years. The venue would become most famous for hosting the finals of the G1 Climax each year, except for a 2014 experiment with a stadium final at the Seibu Dome. It's a natural fit for the most significant tournament in New Japan, and indeed the most respected and intricately booked tournament anywhere in wrestling. While early tournaments were short affairs (the first, won by Keiji Muto over Masahiro Chono took place over a mere four days in August 1991), the modern G1 has fans poring over footage and statistics, speculating about the direction of its two league blocks for an entire month. There's a heavy appeal to mainstream sports fandom that surrounds the G1, making the premier venue for the country's national sport a fine scene for its climax.

Like other sumo halls, Ryogoku is mainly made up of box seats. Similar to cricket in the UK, to the hardcore sumo fan, the sport is an all day affair; attendees show up to watch prelim bouts in the morning and stay all the way up to see the yokozuna in the evening. They often show up with friends, alcohol and a packed lunch, in a communal affair, making the boxed seating arrangement in the building natural; fans sit on cushions laid on the floor, with four adults occupying a single box. People stretch out, stand up, walk around and come back, only really staying for the major bouts at day's end, where major upsets are marked by the cushions being flung into the ring.

For pro wrestling, which requires undivided attention for three or four hours, the boxes are a harder ask on the knees and posterior, especially as the potential for rioting meant no more cushions for the uncivilised wrestling fan to burn and toss. Nevertheless, it's a loud building full of energy, and if any one venue could be considered NJPW's home base, this is it.

Osaka Prefectural Gymnasium

The Osaka Prefectural Gymnasium is one of few buildings that benefitted from corporate sponsorship changing its name. Bodymaker Colosseum, imposed by sponsor BB Sports, carries a wonderful trace of so-called 'Engrish' (to a videogame fan, it evokes memories of Capcom's arcade hit *Saturday Night Slam Masters*, released in Japan as *Muscle Bomber: The Body Explosion*). Osaka in general is famed for hard nosed gangsters rolling their 'r's in the Kansai-ben accent impenetrable to untrained ears, along with comedians, the city turning out more than its fair share of famous TV talent and comics. That said, the Osaka Prefectural Gymnasium has a very serious history in boxing, sumo, and indeed pro wrestling; the gym's 1950 construction makes it the oldest major venue for touring wrestling companies in Japan.

Kansai based promotions like Osaka Pro and Dragon Gate further south in Kobe are often given to Osakan comedy, in turns poking through the fourth wall to make fun of the whole affair and having more serious bouts. When the Kanto groups make their way west, the Osaka crowd turns more serious, vocally supportive, but often with a similarly contrarian, or perhaps trend-setting edge that Korakuen crowds in Tokyo have. The difference is that while 2000 or so fans can often make their presence known by booing someone like Tanahashi, who adapts with relish, some 8000 fill Bodymaker with the same dissenting voice.

It's a voice that was often turned against Tetsuya Naito for one. Perhaps the audience was eager to spark a heel turn for the wild haired star after his return from injury and victory in the 2013 G1 Climax was followed up on poorly and resulted in a lukewarm defeat by Kazuchika Okada at Wrestle Kingdom the following year. Perhaps they were desirous of a harder edge to the strong worker but fairly bland character. Either way, he was roundly booed at every Bodymaker event. It's a phenomenon that baffled even Naito, who was readily cheered nearly everywhere else at the time. He would admit in a 2015 documentary 'it's only me, and only there. I just don't understand it'. When Naito did change his character to that of an uncaring Mexican *rudo* inspired persona, the Osaka crowd booed even more vociferously - this time the reaction was a desired one.

It's that dynamic that sums up Osaka though, and cements the gym as a crucial venue for NJPW. In a country where the (incorrect) perception is that wrestling crowds are muted, it's the Osakan voice that rings most loudly.

7

The Wrestling Bubble

The light that shines twice as brightly only shines half as long, or so the saying goes. When the UWF U Turn of 1985 happened, the ensuing feud was electric, but as we saw earlier, the resulting program was reasonably brief. The stable's de facto leader, Akira Maeda, and his legitimate heat was a major reason for this. Already disliked on his return to the NJPW locker room, he made no attempt to endear himself to his colleagues by being easy to work with. On November 19, 1987, during a six man tag, Riki Choshu had navigated Maeda's stablemate Osamu Kido into a Scorpion Deathlock. Maeda broke up the hold by delivering a brutal kick to Choshu's face, shattering his orbital bone. Maeda was fired, and would reboot the UWF as a promotion proper, the reborn federation being extremely popular and shining brightly in the late 1980s and early 1990s before again, burning half as long as it could have.

Incredibly, Maeda was able to negotiate with Inoki on the release of several established and promising NJPW stars to work in the new UWF. Veteran Yoshiaki Fujiwara was allowed to leave, as was a pair of young prospects in the form of Masakatsu Funaki, and a man who had wrestled Inoki during his 'restart' working in opening matches - Minoru Suzuki. Without Sayama's influence on the new promotion, Maeda was able to push his philosophy on the new company, and its very different approach. In addition to the harder hitting, MMA-esque philosophy, matches only finished by knockout or submission, which guaranteed clean finishes, without the cop-out DQs or count-outs often employed by Inoki to avoid doing the honours for an opponent.

The restarted UWF was immensely popular, and all on the strength of word of mouth. The promotion had no TV deal whatsoever, yet on November 29, 1989 drew 50,000 fans to the Tokyo Dome for their U-Cosmos show, comfortably outdrawing NJPW in the same building earlier that spring.

The strong economy saw a lot of money being thrown in a lot of places in sports and entertainment media. Wrestling was no different, and while the promotions that sprung up during the early '90s were often poorly managed and short lived, they almost all drew impressive crowds. Genichiro Tenryu, a Baba trainee and mainstay of All Japan during the '80s, left his alma mater and formed Super World of Sports, a promotion that had financial backing from, of all places, an eyeglasses chain called Megane Super. Its bizarre origins aside, SWS drew decent crowds to the Dome as well, and Tenryu even managed to forge a decent working relationship with the WWF for a period. When SWS sank, he formed Wrestle and Romance (WAR not, sadly, a battle of lovers and fighters, would rebrand in the mid '90s as Wrestle Association-R, and keep going up to the turn of the millennium).

There was ultraviolence in the form of W*ING, IWA Japan and Atsushi Onita's FMW, all of which later inspiring Paul Heyman's ECW promotion in the States. Women's wrestling hit its peak, with female stars becoming pin-up idols, female role models and powerful, impressive athletes. Truly, wrestling was no longer a genre, but a medium unto itself in Japan, with varied experiences, all of them proving viable (at least from a live drawing perspective).

New and All Japan, by not forcing themselves into a specific niche per se, were able to take note of the rising success of other promotions, lifting their booking philosophies, and, where beneficial, talent for cross promotional purposes. 1990s New Japan saw a definitive move away from count outs and disqualifications, with most matches ending in a clean finish. This might have been a reaction to UWF's popularity, especially as the Russian influence on Superpowers Clash did little to legitimise the product in the eyes of the mainstream, and left fans as mildly baffled as they were for the Willem Ruska/Inoki fights in the '70s. After Shota Chochishvili defeated Inoki at the first Tokyo Dome show, Inoki quietly won back his Real Martial Arts title in May of 1989 at a non-televised event, before transforming the belt into the Greatest 18 championship.

The title, referencing the 'Greatest 18 Club', an NJPW Mount Rushmore-cum-Hall of Fame created by Inoki as part of his thirty year career celebration, was a secondary championship that in theory would be defended in more UWF style MMA themed bouts. In reality, the title lingered in the middle of cards before quietly disappearing altogether, its final champion being Keiji Muto in 1992.

Keiji Muto would drop the Martial Arts championship, but go on to be four time IWGP champion *Photo: Moritsuna Kimura/AFLO*

As the Real Martial Arts championship changed its role within NJPW and was then retired, its creator was taking a greatly diminished role as well. With his political career developing, Inoki would make 1989 his last year as a full time wrestler.

He would spend the following years wrestling in big attraction matches in between failed bids at the Tokyo governor seat and peace tours abroad; in Iraq shortly before the outbreak of the first Gulf War, and most famously in April 1994 in North Korea. There, two shows in Pyongyang headlined by Shinya Hashimoto and Scott Norton, followed by Ric Flair and Inoki would draw 150,000 and 170,000 attendees respectively. Whether those attending completely understood what was happening, or were even there entirely of their own free will in the strict dictatorship is doubtful, but these were legitimately the largest live crowds ever to see professional wrestling.

Along with a diminished in-ring role, Inoki had a smaller part to play behind the scenes as well, handing over most of the booking reigns to VP and long time partner Seiji Sakaguchi. Sakaguchi and Inoki would have their last tag match together at the Dome in February of 1990, defeating Chono and Hashimoto in a match promoted as the two youngsters wanting to end the veterans' era once and for all (this would be prefaced by a famous promo where an Inoki questioned over what would happen if he lost violently slapped the reporter). It was, frankly, a weak main event. Sakaguchi, who would retire from the ring a month later, looked slow, and the finish came quickly and flatly, Inoki landing an enzuigiri and pinning Chono, who kicked out just after the count of three to save face in a bout the younger stars really should have won. It presided over a strong and memorable undercard; surprisingly so considering a lot of it came together at the last minute.

NJPW at this point was at the start of a rocky relationship with World Championship Wrestling that would last through the best part of the decade. The billed main event was to be WCW/NWA champion Ric Flair defending against Keiji Muto making his return to the country. There was a dispute over Flair's proposed payoff, however, and he abandoned the show at the last minute. Sakaguchi hurriedly appealed to All Japan and Baba, who was surprisingly gracious in loaning talent to bulk up the card, the only caveat being that NJPW couldn't beat AJPW in any interpromotional match. This lead to an attractive trio of AJPW and NJPW bouts, along with an undercard that again saw Russian athletes return to New Japan (the most famous being Victor Zangief, though his fame largely came from becoming a visual inspiration for the similarly named Russian wrestler in Capcom's game *Street Fighter* 2 scant months later).

For All Japan, Jumbo Tsuruta and Yoshiaki Yatsu took on former Fujinami partner Kengo Kimura and Osamu Kido. Tiger Mask (played by Mitsuharu Misawa at this point) and Tenryu defeated Riki Choshu and George Takano, who had worked through most of the '80s as a masked Ugandan character called The Cobra (including a series of matches with the original Tiger Mask). Finally, there was a dream foreigner match, as IWGP champion Big Van Vader faced Stan Hansen of AJPW. The ugly brawl that resulted in a double DQ to prevent Vader looking like a weak champion is most memorable for its opening minutes, where Hansen, the wild brawler that also was near blind without corrective lenses, accidentally landed a blow that broke Vader's orbital bone and lead his eye to literally fall from his face. The masked giant was somehow able to pop it back into its socket, where swelling would hold it in place, and the two navigated through a plodding brawl thereafter, but the 53,900 crowd had already been drawn, and Japanese wrestling had been left with an enduring, if disgusting, moment.

If Baba and Sakaguchi managed to successfully get on the same page in order to recover from WCW pulling out in February, the same couldn't be said for the next collaborative effort between the two promotions two months later, a card billed as the US/Japan wrestling summit. This would be an All Japan run return show from the NJPW card just prior, and this time also featured, strangely, WWF stars, thanks to a short relationship between WWF and AJPW, brokered by Tenryu. Despite having some dream matches in the form of Tenryu against Randy Savage, and Hulk Hogan squaring off with Stan Hansen, it was a political mess, and NJPW brass wanted no part in all the cooks spoiling the broth. New Japan's presence was limited, with no cross-promotional matches as Jushin Liger took on Akira Nogami, and Masa Saito and

Shinya Hashimoto defended their IWGP Tag titles against Masahiro Chono and Riki Choshu.

NJPW and WCW mended fences from here, and the two promotions would work together reasonably harmoniously throughout the 1990s, but in truth, NJPW had enough roster depth to carry a strong product on its own. The heavyweight scene in the promotion, now free from the spectre of senior management holding spots in main events, was much more promising, and there were three generations of high quality talent being presented. Choshu and Tatsumi Fujinami represented the 1980s generation; popular veterans with careers spanning three decades at this point with a proven track record. The three musketeers- Chono, Hashimoto, and Muto along with Kensuke Sasaki- these were the new guard, pushing the product forward with innovative stylings and a more character oriented look. Then there was the young guard of dojo graduates, Hiroyoshi Tenzan, Satoshi Kojima, and Yuji Nagata all being stars that would define the company in the latter half of the decade and into the new millennium.

Fujinami, having missed most of 1989 and 1990 with a herniated disc, returned immediately in the main event mix, resuming his long held feud with Riki Choshu over the IWGP Championship, as well as the program with Vader that was interrupted by his injury. Choshu had just regained the title for his second reign after an electric bout with Vader on one of NJPW's first cards back to Ryogoku after their banning in 1987. When Fujinami returned, there was now a trio in the main event mix with a deep history and a decade of emotional investment.

For Fujinami's part, he had his most famous match in March of 1991 as WCW and NJPW presented the joint Tokyo Dome card that was supposed to happen a year prior. He defended the IWGP title against 'NWA' (the lineage of the NWA title gets immensely confusing at this point thanks to WCW's inception, and would get even more convoluted when Flair would leave for the WWF in '91) Champion Ric Flair. Flair/Fujinami would be a double title match under NWA rules, with a red hot crowd of 54,500 in the Dome.

With the huge nationalistic crowd eager to see a clash of Japan and America's best, invoking Gotch and Inoki so long ago, NJPW badly wanted Fujinami crowned champion. In America though, where that belt would be defended most, Fujinami had little to no drawing power. The result was an infamous 'Dusty Finish' named after Dusty Rhodes, who booked WCW at the time. Late in the match, referee Bill Alfonso was struck and tumbled to the outside. In the ring meanwhile, Fujinami evaded a charging Flair and threw him over the top rope to the floor, a disqualification under NWA rules (and a rule so obtuse, it seemed to exist solely for the creation, and ceaseless exploitation of, the Dusty Finish in the first place). Tiger Hattori, the Japanese referee, hopped in the ring and counted three for Fujinami shortly afterward. The Dome crowd went home ecstatic, sure that they'd seen a new champion, but within a week, the 'controversy' would see Flair regain the NWA title, and a double championship match resulted in no titles changing hands.

Despite WCW painting over the finish in their continuity, in New Japan Fujinami was presented as the only person in history to hold both NWA and IWGP championships simultaneously, and despite the asterisk, this achievement was also sold to fans when Fujinami entered the WWE hall of fame in 2015.

Choshu meanwhile, remained in the mix, and worked with Tenryu, of all people, in 1993. After SWS failed, Tenryu's WAR promotion needed financial backing, which cross promotion with NJPW provided, as well as some impressive matches between New and All Japan's bigger stars during the 1980s. Choshu would also play the veteran mentor role to a young up and comer by the name of Takayuki Iizuka, winning the IWGP Tag Championships once. Though Iizuka perhaps didn't live up to the expectations that were put upon him early in his career, he was able to become one of Japanese wrestling's most enduring mainstays, still wrestling today after a change in his first name to Takashi.

Fujinami and Choshu both, while still popular, felt like the gatekeepers to the changing of the guard at this point; in a very real sense in Choshu's regard, as he ascended to the booker role in the early '90s. They were the last truly popular stars in New Japan that had been around in the '70s and bore witness to the shift to a more character driven era. They had seen Tiger Mask become incredibly popular as they were still in plain black trunks, black boots and no kneepads. The three musketeers, then, were stars of the more cosmetic late '80s and '90s. Chono wore long white tights, which made him look more slim and wiry than he was, but set him apart, along with his trademark beard. Muto wore bright orange and neon, making his Great Muta alter ego all the more of a visual spectacle. Hashimoto was the most no-nonsense of the three, but his long martial arts gear and white headband were visual highlights. The point was that these new stars were instantly recognisable at a glance, and used their natural charisma to hold the gaze once it had landed upon them.

These stars were given a new opportunity to further establish themselves in 1991. The G1 Climax, a reimagining of the World League concept from the '70s, was created as a short summer tournament running at first over four days in August. It consisted of eight wrestlers divided into two groups, with the winners of round robin matches facing one another in the final. The tournament would grow over the course of 25 years, changing structure and growing in scope, to the point of G1 Climax 25 taking place over the course of a month and 19 shows.

In '91 though, it existed to put Chono into the forefront. Beating Muto in the final of the first tournament, Chono would win the first two G1s consecutively, and later earn the nickname of 'Mr. August'. The second G1 tournament would be the only one not to have a league structure, instead being a single elimination tournament to crown a new NWA champion (as mentioned, this was where the NWA/WCW title lineage was hazy, after Ric Flair brought the WCW title to the WWF). Chono beat Rick Rude in the '92 finals to become NWA champion, which would be a belt defended internationally on WCW television, but as a secondary championship to the WCW title. Chono had a tough time with the 'big gold belt' in the States more often than not, with lukewarm reactions and matches dominated by crowds chanting 'we want Flair', angry at the former champ's departure.

The NWA title in NJPW was used in much the same way the IWGP Intercontinental Championship is utilised today, or the UN title was in JWA; perhaps a secondary title, but given high billing and almost equal significance. It was, nonetheless, a difficult reign for Chono, made harder in September of 1992 where in a Yokohama Arena title defence against Steve Austin, a sit out Tombstone piledriver left Chono with compressed discs in his neck. It was a scene eerily similar to the incident that would later put Austin on the shelf in 1997 while wrestling Owen Hart, and Chono likely didn't do himself any favours by continuing to work through the injury; including with one Keiji Muto.

Muto was the optimal partner and rival for Chono. Chono was grounded, reasonably no-nonsense and for the time being, clean cut. He had a grounded style, and frequently worked knees in order to look for a finish with his STF. Muto meanwhile was vibrant and high flying, with a lightning fast 'flashing' elbow drop and a visually stunning moonsault that would sadly take the toll on his knees as he advanced in years. The two made a good young tag team in 1990 and '91, particularly against foreign powerhouse teams like the Steiners, whose mix of hard hitting clubbing blows and athleticism made for a popular act when brought over by WCW, or the Road Warriors during their brief run together in NJPW after being popular for Baba in the '80s.

It was as opponents that they were most intriguing though, and it was no mistake that the first G1 Climax built to a Muto/Chono final. What drew fans in most of all about Muto as a singles act was his ability to take on the Great Muta persona, and in so doing embody an entirely different character, with a harder edge; a 'super heel' as announcers called it. He was mystical, other worldly, but somehow not camp in any way; his alter ego helping to providing a pattern for Mick Foley's various faces in his WWF career, as well as more recently Finn Balor (Prince Devitt)'s transformations in WWE.

Muta was wild, imposing, horrific. His legend was undeniably etched in stone in Hiroshima in an autumn 1990 feud with Hiroshi Hase, an early IWGP Junior Heavyweight champion, who had made the transition to heavyweight and was a consistent, if undervalued mid card player through the '90s, working well as a single or teaming with Kensuke Sasaki.

Halfway through their September 14 match Muta sent Hase into the ringpost on the outside, and Hase came up drenched in blood. Whether he had been over enthusiastic in 'getting colour' with a razor blade, or accidentally cut by the post itself, it was a grisly sight, Hase's head wound gushing over his chest. Hase played with the cut to the hilt as a sympathetic babyface, and Muta was equally brilliant, targeting the head with a flashing elbow and cradle, Gotch style, piledriver. Hase showed incredible fire in the latter half of the match, ultimately thrown out after Muta sprayed mist in his opponent's face, symbolically placed Hase on a stretcher and landed a moonsault. This set up a return match in December that year, in which Hase drew blood from Muta. A lot of blood; so much in fact that the 'Muta scale' became the unofficial metric of choice by wrestling pundits as a means of measuring how gruesome a match was.

It's a shame that these matches did more for Muto than they ever did for Hase, who was a capable hand and an appreciated babyface; instead Hase was around, but rarely in the main event mix, before leaving in controversial circumstances in 1995. Hase had recruited Hiromitsu Gompei, a promising amateur wrestler in 1994, but Gompei died of a severe head injury while training in January '95. With Hase unable to get a clear answer from the company as to the circumstances surrounding his death (some placed the blame on Sasaki violently throwing Gompei and attacking him in a bid to motivate the youngster), he left early in 1996 after a Tokyo Dome retirement match with his former partner. He then forged a career in politics, as well as wrestling for All Japan.

As for Muto/Muta, he had the torch passed to him by Choshu himself on August 16 1992, winning his first IWGP championship. Holding the belt for more than a year, he would become the company's longest reigning IWGP champion up to that point, with marquee defenses against The Great Kabuki, Sting, and of course, Chono at the top of the January 4 1993 Tokyo Dome card (NJPW had, in 1992, started their tradition of major cards in the Tokyo Dome on January 4 every year, the first day of trading after the New Year's holiday). It wasn't until September 1993 that he relinquished the belt, to Shinya Hashimoto.

What made the Three Musketeers such an attractive prospect to lead New Japan into the '90s was that they each brought something unique to the table. Chono was grounded and mat based, Muto was high flying and enigmatic, and Hashimoto was no-nonsense and centered his style around striking. His bulk added gravitas to everything that he did, and he was a tremendous counterpoint to the UWF's public trumpeting that they were the only 'real' wrestling promotion in Japan.

Upon winning the IWGP championship from Muta in September 1993, he would have a stranglehold on the belt that would last well into 1995, only interrupted briefly by Fujinami's penultimate title reign. An upset cradle that still gave Hashimoto an 'out' (the referee missed a clear rope break) was redressed the very next month in Hiroshima where Hashimoto destroyed Fujinami in just six minutes and four seconds, delivering a series of head kicks and finally his DDT.

Sting was an interesting product of the WCW relationship, working well with Muto *Photo: Yukio Hiraku/AFLO*

The short main event was a key tool in the eyes of both New and All Japan bookers; used sparingly it created an angered crowd for one night, but one that understood that a finish could come at any time, even in the main event, and to expect the unexpected.

The Fujinami rematch also helped to convince any lingering doubters that Hashimoto was a monster. His multiple defences throughout the following year only intensified as audiences wondered whether anyone could topple him, and whenever Hashimoto sold a chink in his armour the audiences reacted fervently. He would not only strengthen the IWGP championship, as Muto did, by holding onto it for so long, but was also able to help establish his challengers as stars in the fans' eyes even in defeating them.

Kensuke Sasaki was one such performer; the neon-clad long haired citizen of Fukuoka employed a similar clubbing style to Hashimoto's. After toiling for a long time as Power Warrior, tagging with Road Warrior Hawk after partner Animal 'retired' due to injury in 1990, he had his first main event back under his real name with Hashimoto in the Tokyo Dome. Sasaki bloodying Hashimoto's nose and the strong offense he got in helped solidify the return to his old persona as significant in fans' minds, and Sasaki would go on to much success in the second half of the decade.

NJPW may not have had the prime time TV slot they held in the early 1980s, but the strong product still drew big ratings. It wasn't just the present stars at their peak that were popular though, as underneath was the next generation of talent that would help NJPW close the millennium.

After a six year hiatus, the Young Lion Cup returned in 1993, working mainly as a platform to elevate Manabu Nakanishi, Satoshi Kojima and Yuji Nagata. Much like the Three Musketeers at the start of the decade, these three would go onto great things in the latter half of the '90s, a powerhouse, a fiery and brash hard hitter, and an accomplished amateur displaying a variety of suplexes respectively. Joined by Hiroyoshi Tenzan who would alternate between tagging and feuding with Kojima over the years, the future of the heavyweight scene seemed assured for the time being.

Yet for all this, and New Japan still being the popular wrestling choice amidst strong competition, hardcore fans, when pushed, would site All Japan as being a superior heavyweight product. Much as Inoki withdrew from the main event scene in NJPW, so too did Baba in AJPW, and health problems affecting main '80s star Jumbo Tsuruta would necessitate a change to a new generation. Kenta Kobashi, Mitsuharu Misawa, Toshiaki Kawada and Akira Taue would work in various combinations during the '90s in fantastic hard hitting bouts that fans ate up.

In countering this NJPW put an emphasis on the junior division, the innovative lighter high fliers providing something that the AJPW product didn't, and attracting younger fans as well. In-house, Jushin Liger, now adding the 'Thunder' nickname to his persona, led a strong roster of young athletic stars that included Chris Benoit, who evolved past his masked character presented as Dynamite Kid's long lost sibling Pegasus, to become Wild Pegasus. Benoit was in the title mix at the same time as Akira Nogami, Norio Honaga, and a return of the Tiger Mask character after Misawa unmasked in All Japan. The third incarnation wouldn't be held in as fond regard by fans as Koji Kanemoto would be without the mask; he and Shinjiro Otani would lead a new generation of juniors in the second half of the decade.

NJPW became the destination of choice for smaller foreign talent stopping through Japan, and Dean Malenko, Eddie Guerrero and Chris Jericho would all come through New Japan, the working relationship between NJPW and WCW facilitating their move to the big time in America.

Rather than presenting the Junior Heavyweight title as secondary to the IWGP championship, they were instead held as different but nearly equal. Liger was a strong leader for the junior division and adored by fans; this lead to a February 4 1994 double champion match at Budokan hall between Hashimoto and Liger that was billed as a dream bout. Liger's stick and run approach to Hashimoto's tank like power was a sight to see, and importantly the match was a competitive twenty minutes between two champions arguably at the peak of their drawing power.

1994 would prove to be an important year for junior heavyweights across Japan, with NJPW's juniors particularly standing out. That spring saw New Japan host the Super J Cup, a one night tournament in Ryogoku that would see New Japan's top juniors face off against independents and workers from other promotions. Super Delphin and Negro Casas appeared from Mexico, TAKA Michinoku and Great Sasuke came in from Michinoku Pro, and Hayabusa appeared from FMW. It was a rogue's gallery of the very best high fliers in the world, and the knockout tournament won by Benoit over Black Tiger, Gedo (who had moved past his Crush persona with partner Jado (aka Punish) to become mildly more serious but still clad in ridiculous ring gear) and Sasuke, who had a phenomenal night of performances, would be held by many as the greatest single night of wrestling matches in history.

As Wild Pegasus pinned Sasuke with a top rope belly to belly suplex, Ryogoku roaring its approval, both men were made, with Sasuke in particular gaining immense exposure and interest not just in Japan, but internationally for his performance. The success and affirmation that smaller stars could draw big houses that the first Super J Cup provided would see Ultimo Dragon and WAR host a second cup in 1995. It was similarly well received by fans, but interpromotional politics and cost would put paid to it becoming regular. Instead the Cup would be folded into the Best of the Super Juniors tournament hosted by NJPW each summer and predominantly featuring New Japan stars with a few guests.

A decade on from the Anton Hisel scandal leading to a time of upheaval within New Japan, the promotion had recovered from their setbacks and was looking incredibly strong. moving through the mid '90s, we would see a hot angle copied elsewhere, a preponderance of stables, significant retirements, and the Japanese wrestling bubble show signs of popping.

The Greatest 18: Then and Now

In September 1990, Inoki marked the 30th anniversary of his professional debut with a gala dinner and press conference. The dinner was to honour the 'Greatest 18' - the most significant 18 opponents and colleagues of Inoki's career. Given that Inoki himself had organised the party and club (with Lou Thesz as a figurehead commissioner), it was quite the self aggrandizing move (Inoki himself was a member, meaning he effectively inducted himself into his own hall of fame), but created an interesting view into who Inoki believed to be most significant to his career, and by extension, the foundation of NJPW.

The club was, like WWE's current Hall of Fame, caught in a mysterious void between kayfabe and reality, at once oddly honest (many of its entrants were not present for the anniversary dinner and may not have even known of the 'honour' at all at the time but were included nonetheless) and tied to storyline (Tiger Jeet Singh's inclusion in the club came after his 1990 return to New Japan after working for Baba. He'd team with long time rival Inoki to defeat Vader and Animal Hamaguchi on Inoki's thirtieth anniversary card, but after he predictably went back to his evil ways to work with Hiroshi Hase, Inoki 'expelled' him from the group, replacing him with Dusty Rhodes). What makes it an intriguing piece of history though, is that it was a locked off group of 18, and apart from the Tiger Jeet Singh switch, was never to be added to or subtracted from. With the benefit of hindsight, and in the post Inoki era of NJPW, who would be in the club if it existed today? Here we will take a look at the original club members (discounting Inoki himself), and consider a Greatest 18 of the modern age.

THE ORIGINAL 18

Lou Thesz

Thesz was well into his fifties by the time NJPW was founded, meaning that he only worked for Inoki a total of three times, twice with the founder (as part of a tag match with Karl Gotch, and with Seiji Sakaguchi as Inoki's partner, followed by an NWF title match in October 1975) and once with Masahiro Chono at age 74 in more of an angle and publicity stunt than a match. While certainly not youthful looking when working with Inoki, he was still an effective foil for the NWF champion approaching the peak of his popularity and effectively displayed the grappling game and charisma that earned him six NWA world championships.

By this point though, Thesz had already reached legendary status, and his position within NJPW history was as a result of the respect Inoki had for a founding father of wrestling in Japan, and his seminal role in mentor Rikidozan's career. Inoki and Thesz worked together just under two decades on from Thesz's immensely popular run with Rikidozan in JWA, which set television viewing records that will never be matched again.

Karl Gotch

Inoki's dealings with Karl Gotch in New Japan were rather more frequent than with Thesz, the pair facing off against one another eight times over the first couple of years of the promotion.

This speaks to Gotch's bond to Inoki, and the helping hand he lent during the promotion's unstable beginnings. By working with Inoki out of the gate (in NJPW's first main event, no less) and helping to book the American talent he was close with in NJPW's nascent pre-television days, he was able to help secure a future for the promotion. When NJPW did gain a television spot, it was Gotch who wrestled Inoki for the new Real World Heavyweight Championship, and drew strong enough ratings to ensure survival.

As a trainer, meanwhile, Gotch was able to impart sound fundamentals and punishing mat work. He helped immensely in creating what NJPW would sell as 'Strong Style', and as a result would have a tournament named in his honour to celebrate younger stars from 1974-1976. While the inaugural winner of said tournament, Tatsumi Fujinami, would undoubtedly become the most famous of its champions, Yoshiaki Fujiwara and Shoji Kai would both have long running and influential careers that were testament to Gotch's significance.

Nick Bockwinkel

Nick Bockwinkel seemed an unusual choice for inclusion in the group, at least based on his work in New Japan. Bockwinkel hadn't wrestled for the promotion, and his presence at the dinner seemed to simply serve as a prelude to the former AWA champion serving as special guest referee for Inoki's tag match in the associated show. His ties to the AWA meant that up until his 1987 semi-retirement he would work for All, not New, Japan when in the country.

You have to look back to before New Japan's foundation to see the two crossing paths on Japanese soil. In late 1970, JWA ran a cross promotional tag team tournament with the NWA, which Inoki won alongside fellow Rikidozan trainee Kantaro Hoshino. Nick Bockwinkel and Joe Quinn fell to the Japanese tandem in the final, and shortly afterward Inoki would be elevated with a run with the newly created NWA UN title.

The inductees to the Greatest 18 club were of course hand picked by Inoki himself, and personal leanings and friendships may have taken precedence over historical significance when picking Bockwinkel.

Johnny Powers

Inoki's admiration for Lou Thesz undoubtedly help pave the way for a long NJPW career for Johnny Powers, who trained under Thesz before forging a career in the Detroit area. He would become a mainstay in New Japan through much of the 1970s, a relationship that began when Inoki was struggling to enter NJPW into the NWA. Powers was running his own promotion, the NWF in the States, and arranged a working relationship with Inoki that would secure a steady stream of foreign talent for New Japan. It would also result in the NWF Heavyweight championship being recognised as NJPW's major title, before Powers would sell his company outright to Inoki.

The two had a significant business relationship behind the scenes, then, but would also work with one another extensively in-ring, and often over that NWF championship. Inoki beat Powers for the belt on December 10, 1973, and would retain for well over a year before starting his long feud with Tiger jeet Singh.

Powers was a respected hand in the ring, but it's the NWF/NJPW merger that made his role in Inoki's history most important. It would provide a route for foreign talent when the company wasn't in the NWA, as well as a championship with supposed international prestige.

Johnny Valentine

Johnny Valentine's time in New Japan was brief. In 1975, Valentine found himself in the same plane crash that famously broke Ric Flair's back. Valentine himself would be paralysed, ending his in-ring involvement in wrestling. He was, however, significant in Inoki's career for his time with the short-lived Tokyo Pro Wrestling. Former JWA executive Toyonobori, on exiting the company on bad terms, had convinced Inoki to join him in creating a new promotion with Inoki as its main star. The company was hamstrung by a lack of foreign talent, but Valentine took the chance of working with Toyonobori, and losing to Inoki in the promotion's first main event. This was no minor gesture, as it could easily have harmed Valentine's standing with the NWA who were working with the JWA at the time. It was a move Inoki would remember well.

Andre The Giant

Andre the Giant would come into NJPW in 1974 via the NWF relationship, and would remain a presence in New Japan all the way into the mid 1980s, even as he grew to super stardom in the WWF. Andre was increasingly limited in the ring during his final runs with New Japan, garnering quick victories over the likes of Inoki and Seiji Sakaguchi in brief singles matches, or working in six man tags. When contesting for the NWF title in 1974 and '75 however, Andre was surprisingly mobile, and created an exciting David and Goliath dynamic in his bouts with Inoki, smothering his smaller opponent for the most part and willing to take dramatic spills over the top rope when necessary.

Andre was, naturally, an easily marketable star as NJPW was attracting more foreign talent. He instantly leapt out as a huge imposing figure, and would be booked to serve that character well. It was also a feather in

Inoki's cap that he was able to retain Andre even while engaged in a bidding war over foreign talent with Baba. Baba undoubtedly would have wanted a big singles match spectacle with Andre, something ultimately denied fans. Neither star was capable of a singles feud when Andre did appear in AJPW in 1990, and the two mainly found themselves on opposite sides of six man tags until Andre's final Japanese appearance in 1992, and death in 1993.

Tiger Jeet Singh

Purely from the perspective of most time worked with one another, Tiger Jeet Singh is the most significant foreign member of Inoki's 18. He was also significant as a foreign character that was built in New Japan, as opposed to coming in with an established legacy elsewhere. While not the most accomplished in-ring technician, his exceptional heel work and the character Jagjeet Singh Hans so whole heartedly dove into made him unforgettable.

Singh was also part of an interesting developmental stage for Inoki as a wrestler and NJPW as a company. The two would feud in a decidedly American influenced, angle driven style, as matches would be interrupted, disqualifications ensued in force, and things even spilled out of the ring, with Singh 'assaulting' Inoki and his wife at a shopping center to build their first NWF title match. Even Singh's entry and subsequent expulsion from the 18 was driven by storyline, and showed the dissonance that existed through Inoki's career as a wrestler and promoter. Inoki's ability to work in this setting as well as drive the self serious-nature of the Martial Arts championship and Muhammad Ali fight to (commercial, if not critical or long term) success was testament to his versatility as a performer. It would also exemplify the push and pull that would harm the company by the early 2000s.

Dusty Rhodes

Dusty Rhodes was fairly prolific in his work with New Japan in the late '70s and early '80s. His high standing within the NWA made him an interesting figure during the bidding wars for foreign talent between All and New Japan. A poor relationship with Baba would lead to him staying with Inoki through to 1984, and when Inoki secured Dick Murdoch in 1981, the pair reformed the Texas Outlaws tag team that drove Dusty to prominence as a heel in the late 1960s. At this point, Rhodes was working as a babyface in Japan with Murdoch following suit, but the dynamic of the Rhodes and Inoki NWF title matches in the late '70s was quite different.

While still billed as the American Dream, this made him a brash foreign heel rather than a relatable blue collar hero in Japan. It's somewhat strange to watch the hero for the masses beg off against a furious Inoki in their November 1 1979 match, holding onto ropes for leverage and bumping the referee to get disqualified. He would be loved by the fans by the time of his exit from the company in 1984 however, and the burgeoning working relationship with WCW by 1990 was also a determining factor in Rhodes' inclusion in the 18.

Stan Hansen

Stan Hansen's program with Inoki was cut short after a sudden hop to All Japan, directly into a feud with Giant Baba. It's his work there that he became most famous for, and where his legacy would match or even best those of Thesz, Gotch and Robinson in the country, easily making him the medium's most famous foreign star in Japan.

At the time of the club's creation in autumn of 1990, Hansen had entered an NJPW ring for the first time in almost a decade thanks to Baba loaning the Texan for the Super Fight Tokyo Dome card. Hansen would also work a handful of times for Inoki that summer, which led storyline credence to his inclusion in the 18.

However, it was for that Inoki feud through 1980 that his NJPW career should be best remembered. Inoki did well to quickly establish Hansen as a threat with a count out loss, and the two would go on to have an exciting series with a well developed in-ring story.

Bill Robinson

Bill Robinson created a classic with Inoki in the December of 1975, but it was his work as a trainer that cemented his legacy in New Japan. The large hand he had in the development of many dojo entrants in the seventies, and his training of the likes of Yoshiaki Fujiwara in the UK helped drive not only the hybrid Strong Style in New Japan, but also the shoot oriented stylings of UWF. As UWF evolved through its different incarnations and on into Pancrase and PRIDE, Robinson was a key figure in the development of pro wrestling and of mixed martial arts, the two loves that conflicted Inoki so.

Willem Ruska

Willem Ruska exists in a strange place in Inoki's and NJPW's history. Working on and off for the company for five years between 1976 and 1980, the judoka never seemed particularly comfortable in a pro wrestling ring, and proved a challenging opponent for most to produce an exciting match with. He wasn't brought in by Inoki as a pro wrestler, however, but on the strengths of his Olympic accomplishments in judo, supposedly making him a fine first challenger for the newly created Martial Arts championship, on the way to building the Ali affair.

Had the trio of bouts between Ruska and Inoki in 1976 been legitimate fights, they may have been more entertaining, but would also have ended in short order in Ruska's favour. The worked bouts they did have were awkward affairs, but in presenting the clash of fighting styles, served as a key point in the early days of MMA.

Muhammad Ali

If the Ruska bouts were somewhat clumsy, the Ali fight was a disaster. The confusing, plodding bout mired in inter-camp politics was one of combat sports' most infamous duds. The cost involved in laying on the match would mean it wasn't a financial success either, but in terms of pure number of eyes on the ring in Japan and abroad, was the most famous of Inoki's matches by some margin. It may have been an hour of kicks to the shins that put an audience of millions to sleep, but it was also the height of Inoki's celebrity up to that point, and made Ali undoubtedly a significant opponent for the NJPW founder.

Hiro Matsuda

Another Rikidozan trainee, Hiro Matsuda would forge a successful career in the US as a wrestler and feared but respected trainer of Hulk Hogan, Lex Luger, Scott Hall and more besides. He was a close friend of Inoki's though, and the two would periodically tag in the JWA before Inoki brought Matsuda into NJPW as one of many independent guests filling out the Pre Japan tournament in 1978. The two would meet in the knockout phase of that tournament, with Inoki naturally winning, and Matsuda would periodically work for NJPW through the early 1980s in between spells in the US. His relationship with Inoki allowed for several of his foreign trainees to come through NJPW's doors, and, in giving Hulk Hogan New Japan bookings despite working for the AWA at the time, helped ease Hogan's return to, and meteoric rise in, the WWF.

Bob Backlund

Inoki's phantom week long WWF title reign was a result of a pair of Backlund matches in the tail end of 1979. Backlund would be part of the WWF's Japanese delegation through to the mid 1980s as well, making his a larger contribution to NJPW history than first appears. His straight-laced clean-cut persona made him a respectable figure in the audience's minds, and with any heat in the WWF title angle solidly put on Tiger Jeet Singh, Backlund would side with Inoki as often as work against him.

With Tatsumi Fujinami being associated with another WWF title (the Junior Heavyweight championship) in the late '70s, Backlund was an easy choice for an early opponent when Fujinami stepped up to heavyweight. Backlund worked as well with inoki's protege as with the founder himself, though a New Year's Day bout in 1982 for the WWF title was stopped short, Fujinami unable to escape a cradle that wasn't the planned finish before the count of three, and confusion reigning in Korakuen Hall. Cannily, Backlund refused to have his hand raised after the unplanned finish, showing the commitment to character that made him a well liked star among the audience, and with Inoki himself.

Verne Gagne

Verne Gagne is the most unusual member of the original Greatest 18. Inoki had teamed up with, or wrestled against, every single other member in the club, but not Gagne. In Japan, Gagne's relationship with Baba and All Japan precluded that from ever happening. In America, meanwhile, the two's paths never crossed in any meaningful way. The closest connection from an in-ring perspective to Gagne was his work with Nick Bockwinkel, the ace of AWA for a long period, and Inoki did very little work with him.

Gagne's inclusion is more of a political one than anything else, then. Gagne wasn't in attendance at the club's dinner (for the record, neither were Ali, Hogan, Backlund, Gotch or Kobayashi) and may not have been aware of his induction. Nevertheless, with the AWA effectively defunct at this point (their last TV show had aired a month prior, and bankruptcy proceedings would take place in 1991), there was a nod being made to the influence Gagne's promotion once had in both the US and Japan, and a potential olive branch for business dealings since the All Japan relationship died when AWA did.

Strong Kobayashi

Strong Kobayashi was a rare hot free agent in contemporary Japanese wrestling on leaving IWE in 1974. Joining NJPW, he could have been slotted into the usual mix working with foreigners on the mid cards underneath Inoki. The founder, however, experimented with an all Japanese main event program with himself and Kobayashi unseen at this level since the Kimura and Rikidozan affair in JWA. Their March 19, 1974 match was promoted as a dream clash of the country's biggest draws, and the promoter's hyperbole wasn't far off the mark, given that the Inoki versus Baba bout Antonio had pushed hard for before leaving JWA was never going to happen. Kuramae Sumo Hall was packed to the rafters with an electric atmosphere, the hot crowd chanting and beating on drums to create the kind of atmosphere usually seen at a baseball match, not a wrestling one.

The match was as hot as the crowd. Mat work transitioned into the pair exchanging open handed blows and then fists, Kobayashi drawing colour from Inoki on the floor to send the crowd into a fever pitch before Inoki was triumphant with a German suplex paying homage to Gotch. As they went through a similarly hot rematch later in the year, the seeds were planted in Inoki's mind to later break away from the accepted format of 'Japan versus the world' and build up a deeper domestic roster. Kobayashi meanwhile would be a featured star for years to come, and do noteworthy heel work as part of the *Shin Kokusai Gundan* in the early 1980s.

Hulk Hogan

It might have been a happy accident for his part that Inoki lost the finals of the inaugural IWGP tournament, but through his victory, Hulk Hogan became a big star for NJPW and in the Japanese mainstream. His look, and a higher work rate than in American territories with their more demanding travel schedules earned him endorsements, and made him a true star, foreshadowing his subsequent success in the US. Inoki would of course get his win back on Hogan in due course, but a star had been made.

Seiji Sakaguchi

The final member of the original 18 was the closest of all to Inoki. Seiji Sakaguchi would hop from what was left of the struggling JWA to New Japan shortly after its foundation, and become Inoki's right hand man in and out of the ring. In singles matches through to the end of the '70s and into the '80s, Sakaguchi was a solid number two to Inoki; as a tag team they were dominant. Behind the scenes meanwhile, Sakaguchi was vice president, trainer and booker. On entering the Greatest 18 club, Sakaguchi had retired from the ring, but was even more involved as head booker with the company's operations, and before handing over the reigns to Riki Choshu, was at the helm of the bustling and profitable early Tokyo Dome era.

THE NEW 18

This more modern Greatest 18 looks to cement a list of figures that shaped what NJPW is today. Both current and former names, in-ring performers and back office figures, the contributions of this group should not be ignored.

Seiji Sakaguchi
Bill Robinson
Karl Gotch
Antonio Inoki

They key roles of Gotch, Robinson, Sakaguchi and Inoki himself in the story of New Japan make them easily worthy of entry to both old and new clubs. Without the Gotch and Inoki alliance, New Japan could easily have folded as quickly as Tokyo Pro Wrestling did in the '60s. Sakaguchi would be a key ally for Inoki from his defection from JWA, bringing much needed domestic depth to NJPW's roster. Meanwhile stylistically, all were key in the creation and development of what came to be branded as Strong Style.

Inoki, of course, is still synonymous in Japan with pro wrestling and NJPW, even approaching a decade since his family was last involved with the company. Inoki changed the face of the industry in Japan, making celebrities of his talent (and himself) and a household name of his promotion in the changing landscape of the 1980s economic bubble. As aggressively self-promoting as he was in and out of the ring, he was a phenomenal talent with immense charisma. As bizarre (and later, arguably toxic) as some of his ideas were as a promoter and booker, he was innovative and instrumental in the modern production not just of wrestling in Japan, but MMA worldwide.

Hisashi Shinma

While not a wrestler, Hisashi Shinma's significance to the formative years of NJPW and Inoki's career as a promoter would have sealed his entrance into the original 18 were it not for the politics and ill will surrounding his departure in 1984.

Shinma was a key figure in NJPW's acceptance into the NWA. With Inoki banned from sitting on the board, Shinma was a middle man that forged key connections with others in the Alliance, most significantly Vince McMahon Senior. It was Shinma that was the driving force behind the NWA and WWF relationships in the late seventies and early eighties. He helped the Inoki/ Ali fight get broadcasted on closed circuit internationally and brought a wave of WWF talent to Japan that otherwise would have been ensnared by Baba and AJPW. He was a key advocate of the junior heavyweights as well, and was instrumental in Tatsumi Fujinami all but adopting the WWF Junior Heavyweight title as an NJPW belt, as well as in the transformation of Satoru Sayama into the original Tiger Mask.

Fired in the wake of the Anton Hisel scandal, the anger Shinma felt was transformed into the creation of the UWF, which did much in itself to transform wrestling and MMA. As an instrumental business figure, Shinma should be in the club.

Tatsumi Fujinami

Tatsumi Fujinami was vital to New Japan for being the first real post Inoki 'ace' of the promotion. In NJPW's formative years, there may have been some degree of roster depth, but on the Japanese side of the roster, it was always Inoki, Sakaguchi, and then everyone else toiling away underneath. Fujinami was a trainee of Inoki's, but his ascent was not born purely out of nepotism. His rise from young prodigy to main eventer was organic, and a result of a long journey through his seminal role in the junior heavyweight division to the feud with Riki Choshu that made stars of both.

Fujinami's loyalty to Inoki and New Japan was key in the wake of the mid 1980s scandals, and duly rewarded with a passing of the torch as Inoki's in-ring role gradually diminished. When it came time to end his own in-ring career, he would take on the rarely envied presidential reins of the company for a five year spell, and arguably would have a position for life had it not been for creative differences with his biggest in-ring rival during the tail end of Simon Inoki's presence and the pit of NJPW's economic valley.

Riki Choshu

Choshu and Fujinami have a complicated relationship with one another, an affair that's marked out with a genuine love and hate, largely dependent on how much money they were making with one another. Choshu's rise to the top of the card in NJPW was somewhat overshadowed by Fujinami's idol status, and it's easy to imagine a certain degree of real life angst playing into their feud through 1983. As Fujinami stayed in New Japan through the scandals and exoduses to All Japan and UWF, Choshu left, and his return in 1987 was born more out of financial motives than ethics or loyalty.

However, Choshu, like Fujinami, was a phenomenal talent. His hard hitting style, plain talking and famous entrance music earned him iconic status (and made him an easy target for parody - comedian *Ko*riki Choshu, who gently lampoons the legend in TV segments as the 'Power Hall' theme plays as a bed underneath, became arguably more famous than his inspiration in the mid 2000s). In his booking role, he helped with the presentation of the immensely successful mid '90s UWFi feud, and even as his decisions grew more erratic in the early 2000s, he was able to come up with some magic, especially in booking pet projects like Kensuke Sasaki.

Jushin Liger

Keiichi Yamada took what was originally intended to be a cash-in licensed property to gain kids' interest in NJPW and a new TV Asahi anime, and turned it into a character that dramatically surpassed its inspiration in every way. He turned a goofy superhero into a gimmick that has lasted for well over half of NJPW's existence as a company, and an iconic representation of wrestling to fans at home and abroad, where Liger is still one of NJPW's most in-demand talents. He was an innovative risk taker and an expert storyteller, and his in-ring achievements can't be understated.

Yet Liger has also been a mentor, trainer and ambassador for his weight class, his promotion and his medium. The influence and respect Yamada commanded resulted in the Super J Cup and the J Crown, two concepts that unified wrestling promotions that ordinarily would have nothing to do with one another for unprecedented cross-promotional matchups. He stayed in New Japan's dojo in Oita for decades after his graduation and progression to bigger things, helping with younger talent, in a role he maintains to this day.

Masahiro Chono
Shinya Hashimoto
Keiji Muto

The Three Musketeers were all phenomenal talents, and each played a unique role in transitioning NJPW from the Inoki, Fujinami and Choshu dominated '80s to the '90s Tokyo Dome era. Each would have their own part in shaping wrestling as a whole in Japan.

Shinya Hashimoto projected a hard-nosed, legitimate aura much needed in a time that the new UWF and the nascent field of mixed martial arts were serious competition.

In the early 1990s, close to a decade of Inoki title feuds with cop-out count out and DQ finishes to half-heartedly establish competitors lingered in the memory. Hashimoto's historic 489 day title reign was marked with consistent clean victories in believable, dramatic matches. With everyone from Muto to Sasaki, and even Jushin Liger, Hashimoto was dramatic, fearsome and showed an athleticism belying his portly stature.

Toward the end of his NJPW run, Hashimoto recognized the crowded nature of the wrestling space in an economy heading for failure. His Zero 'super indie', under NJPW's umbrella, could conceivably have bolstered the company's roster of traditional pro wrestling talent while MMA experiments continued. With the idea squashed and Hashimoto forced out, Zero One had a flying start as its own separate entity. While it was beginning to falter at the time of Hashimoto's passing, thawing relationships with New Japan could easily have seen the company gain a new lease on life, and Hashimoto gain a proper farewell.

Keiji Muto had the easiest natural charisma of the three, and the dynamic between himself and the dark, Great Kabuki inspired, Muta character gave him the biggest legacy of the trio internationally. Muto's versatility as a performer, an athletic technician with Chono or a bloodthirsty demon with Hiroshi Hase, was unmatched, and allowed for a transition into a different style of working by the late 1990s when years of moonsaults destroyed his knees.

Muto was a casualty of the early 2000s vale tudo era. Frustrated at the flirtation with MMA that he felt led to dangerous fights, he would jump to All Japan, becoming company president and later leaving to form Wrestle-1. His creative output away from the ring would struggle to match the art he created within it, but on his returns for occasional matches in the promotion that made him, fan nostalgia was definitely well placed.

Finally, Masahiro Chono. He only ever held the IWGP championship once during his career, and then for a brief reign in 1998 before long brewing neck issues forced him to relinquish it. Yet Chono was a masterful ring general, and in his transformation into a darker alter ego and subsequent formation of nWo Japan, a compelling character to boot. He exuded the 'cool heel' charisma that was the nWo image to a tee, and from his look to his ring style stood out in a crowded roster at the time bloated by cross promotional angles.

Away from the ring, his spell with the NJPW book during Riki Choshu's enforced departure showed some strong traditional storytelling (as in the culmination of Hiroshi Tenzan's journey to the IWGP title) albeit constrained by the desire from higher up to push the company's vale tudo agenda.

As a trio, you'd be hard pressed to find a group of more accomplished performers anywhere at any time. As part of company history, they were vital.

Hiroshi Tanahashi

Being a devotee of, and endorsed by, Tatsumi Fujinami is already a highly pressured position to be in when making your first forays onto the main card in New Japan. Being branded a 'New Musketeer', fans making connections with the heelish work of Keiji Muto early in his career would have added to that pressure on Tanahashi. Moreover, Tanahashi was earmarked as a great hope for the company moving forward while in the deep descent of the early to mid 2000s.

When faux MMA dominated main events, Tanahashi's undercard performances with his U-30 championship offered something different, and showed his potential. Yet his first reign with the IWGP Championship in 2006 came when business for NJPW was at its lowest ebb, and began poorly, with a hastily slapped together tournament after the promotion couldn't retain the services of champion Brock Lesnar long enough for him to do the honours to Tanahashi properly.

Tanahashi could easily have buckled, but he didn't. He would step out of the shadow of audience expectations, exceed them as an arrogant self obsessed heel, earn renewed audience respect in his 2007 battles with Yuji Nagata, and be the centerpiece of NJPW's economic recovery.

While business and booking changes helped, Tanahashi's performances, and the personable face he put forward for the company in the mainstream made him an indispensable resource and incomparable artist.

Shinsuke Nakamura

Tanahashi was in a position of great responsibility during the business downturn, and shouldered the company through the mid 2000s. Shinsuke Nakamura meanwhile was never even groomed for that burden, instead being pushed to the IWGP title and labelled the top guy at the age of just 23.

The faith that Inoki had in Nakamura as he trained under him and Hashimoto in the LA dojo alongside Lyoto Machida would ultimately prove well placed, but it was a long road to hew. Nakamura and Machida both, it was planned, would bridge the gap between MMA and pro wrestling, hopping back and forth and being dominant in both. Ultimately it was an impractical plan, and while Nakamura's brief MMA career was broadly successful, he followed his passions into a wholly pro wrestling focus while Machida would follow his heart into the UFC. While the IWGP title reign under his shooter persona was brief, plagued with injury and not exceptional at the box office, Nakamura showed a rare charisma that fell in line with fan's beliefs that he could be the next Hashimoto of the New Three Musketeers with Tanahashi and Katsuyori Shibata.

Despite his legitimate fighting success and jiu jitsu competency though, Nakamura would tap into his charisma and constantly reinvent himself to gain more of a Muto mystique than a Hashimoto-esque hard nosed nature. Today he is unquestionably NJPW's biggest draw internationally, and presentationally unlike anyone else in the entire medium.

Takaaki Kidani

If and when the final story of New Japan can be told, It's uncertain whether Kidani will be portrayed as a hero or villain. What is clear for now is that his influence on the company will make him a key figure in years to come.

Kidani seemed at first to be a big fan flushed with cash, rather than someone with a game plan to turn a struggling company around. Citing Vince McMahon and Eric Bischoff as his business inspirations, he was keen at the outset to project himself onto the promotion his company Bushiroad purchased in 2012. He brought Kazushi Sakuraba and Katsuyori Shibata back to the promotion without company say-so or even awareness, and rumors gathered that he wanted to turn himself into a regular character on shows.

Yet Kidani, along with Naoki Sugabayashi who had been promoted from president to chairman, also dramatically cut costs, reduced unnecessary domestic touring and pushed hard internationally. 'I have no doubt that our in-ring product is the best in the world, but that the way we do business hasn't moved on for decades', he'd state at a 2015 press conference, talking about a multi-stage program to bring the company to global prominence. His experience in marketing merchandise and intellectual property to younger demographics would translate to a broadening audience for New Japan, sold out shows and improved merchandise sales.

It's the end game for Kidani to potentially turn NJPW public that seems risky, and another case of Kidani patterning himself on McMahon and WWE.

There are large question marks over the future of New Japan, and Kidani may well be the figure that brings the company to glory or destruction.

Kensuke Sasaki

A good deal of Kensuke Sasaki's success in New Japan and wrestling at large might well be due to the influence of friend and mentor Riki Choshu, who made Sasaki a personal project while booking the company in the mid 1990s. Nevertheless, his violent style and gruff persona made him a huge star in his own right, and a mainstream celebrity in Japan today.

Sasaki and Hase complemented one another superbly as a team *Photo: Yukio Hiraku/AFLO*

Entering NJPW as Choshu made his 1987 return to the company, Sasaki would connect with the audience by teaming with Hiroshi Hase in the early '90s. Hase was turning heavyweight after being an early IWGP Junior Heavyweight champion, and was excellent sympathetic foil to Sasaki's brutal tank-like nature. It helped that the NJPW relationship with WCW was developing at this point, which added depth to the tag team roster, and allowed for a string of fantastic matches in Japan and the US with the Steiners.

Sasaki would find his relationship with Hase strained after his rumoured involvement in the death of dojo trainee Hiromitsu Gompei, whom Hase had personally scouted and vouched for. His strong singles push from 1996, as he dropped the Power Warrior persona developed for a tag team run with Road Warrior Hawk, was not without controversy. He was pushed relentlessly hard however, winning the G1 Climax, becoming an IWGP Tag Champion with UWF alum Kazuo Yamazaki, and ending Hashimoto's record IWGP title reign in the space of a month.

His in-ring performances were up to the task. After Hashimoto had been built for a year and a half as an immoveable object, Sasaki was arguably the only credible unstoppable force to transition the title to, and fans ate his modern version of Choshu's Strong Style up. When the opportunity for a dream series with All Japan's Toshiaki Kawada came up, fans clamoured to the Tokyo Dome twice for one of the most significant and fondly remembered angles in company history.

Sasaki was always indebted to Choshu for his success, and the two were inseparable, down to his leaving in 2002 not long after his mentor's firing. His contributions still can't be ignored.

Yuji Nagata

You would be hard pressed to find a better all round talent in NJPW's history than Yuji Nagata. As versatile and impressive a talent as he is though, Nagata is most deserving of inclusion in this Greatest 18 club due to reaching a career peak and carrying the company through an extremely tough period.

Nagata, extremely promising when showing his amateur credentials as a young wrestler during the UWFi program, would do a lot of learning and development in America for WCW while NJPW was at the tail end of the '90s boom.

Nagata was a hugely respected champion during New Japan's toughest years financially. *Photo: Yukio Hiraku/AFLO*

When he came back, the company was transforming, and when he was a top contender and indeed IWGP champion, it was a reign marred by bizarre booking. His reputation and career longevity were threatened by a poor MMA career, including a mauling at the hands of Mirko Cro Cop, and his opponents at the top of the card ran the gamut from accomplished workers to moonlighting fighters who couldn't carry their half of the bargain.

Ultimately though, Nagata was able to weather the storm, and while the late 2000s marked a beginning of his descent down the card, he would establish Hiroshi Tanahashi as the promotion's next ace in the process. His loyalty to the company through adversity, and ability to represent traditional storytelling and stability during a changeable era makes him one of the most respected figures in company history.

Gedo

Keiji Takayama's NJPW career is inextricably linked with that of partner Shoji Akiyoshi (better known as Jado). Though the two spend the occasional time apart, they've mainly been a package deal from their NJPW debuts through FMW, WAR and W*ING for more than 25 years. As a tag team, first Crush and Punish and then as Jado and Gedo, they both went from stable toughs to tag team champions to comedy sidekicks. It's the mark both, but particularly Gedo, has left creatively on NJPW that warrants inclusion here.

Gedo could easily have left NJPW in 2007. He had been offered a lucrative contract with WWE, and New Japan, even in the wake of costs being cut after Yuke's purchased the company was still without sound leadership or firm financial footing.

Gedo, balking at the prospect of playing to national stereotypes for WWE, elected to stay, and as Riki Choshu left his position as booker, New Japan handed the pencil to him and Jado. Between them the pair set about overhauling a roster that had largely been presented homogeneously. In so doing, they brought younger and broader audiences interested in more diverse characters. From new creations, like the brash *nouveau riche* of Kazuchika Okada as the Rainmaker, to transforming Toru Yano and Takashi Iizuka from serious amateur wrestlers to brawlers with comic personalities, they gave reason for emotional investment in every roster member.

As Jado grew more involved assisting in booking Pro Wrestling NOAH, it was Gedo that continued to show his skill. He'd establish newcomers to the company like AJ Styles and Michael Elgin with the Japanese audience with strong booking in successive G1 tournaments, and continue to intricately program the G1 as a whole, establishing it, and the January 4 Tokyo Dome show it set up, as Japan's premier seasons to mark on the wrestling calendar.

Tiger Hattori

Masao 'Tiger' Hattori's role in New Japan today is similar to that of Hisashi Shinma back in the 70's and 80's. Splitting his time between Tokyo and New York, he's a key international liaison, working to book Japanese talents in the U.S. for partners like ROH and allowing foreign talents to find a home in NJPW (Young Lion Jay White, for example, would find a spot in the New Japan dojo after being introduced by Fergal 'Prince' Devitt).

Hattori also still works as a referee, and has done for close to forty years. He would begin his refereeing career in the States, before working with All Japan as an NWA sanctioned ref. He would have an on again, off again relationship within NJPW, working during the early 1980s and again sporadically through the 90s (he would be the Japanese referee for the Fujinami/ Ric Flair NWA title match), before finding his current position in 2004, making use of four decades of experience and connections to help forge an international path for the company.

8

Invasion Attack

NJPW and UWF would find their paths crossing once more in 1995, but this was a different promotion again to the one that set up shop in 1984 and in '88. The Akira Maeda led incarnation of UWF closed in October 1990, barely a year after its huge Tokyo Dome show.

Creative differences and financial issues scuppered the company. Akira Maeda would go on to form another pseudo MMA promotion in the form of RINGS, Masakatsu Funaki and Minoru Suzuki formed pure MMA company Pancrase, and the remaining talent headed by top star Nobuhiko Takada span off into Union of Wrestling Forces International, UWFi.

UWFi, built around Takada and with a strong undercard that included a young Kazushi Sakuraba before becoming the 'Gracie Hunter' in the PRIDE years, was still a popular cult promotion. In what is rarely a good idea for a wrestling company though, it would earn brief notoriety by directly referencing rivals; Takada would often label All and New Japan as fake (it was) while UWFi was the real deal (it wasn't). Open challenges would be offered to other companies that would be summarily ignored. Only WCW and Vader would agree to a handsome fee to put Takada over; at this point Vader was working less in Japan anyway, and it was hardly as if a loss for their champion in the Far East (before the days of social media making embarrassments very public) was a big deal. The irony of the whole situation was that a decade later, after his pro wrestling career transitioned into a run in MMA, Takada would become one of Japanese wrestling's goofiest characters, the leader of the Takada Monster Army in the cartoonish 'fighting opera' promotion Hustle.

The adage of not throwing stones from glass houses was being proven in 1994 and 1995, as UWFi's derision of other companies wasn't having a hugely positive impact at the box office, and the company was drowning in debt. The temporary solution was to build a bridge with New Japan. UWFi management approached Riki Choshu with the idea of their talent working in New Japan; NJPW had creative control on the angle while helping fund the struggling company.

As a result, NJPW was 'invaded' by UWFi in August 1995. It was slightly different from the prior invasion angles in the company; unlike in the '80s with IWE and the original UWF, the invading forces here were part of a company that was legitimately still operating. It added a layer of authenticity to the idea of a company under attack, and meant for incredibly hot cards in Ryogoku and the Tokyo Dome.

It was a good thing outside intrigue played its part, since for the most part Choshu took the creative control card and used it to make his stars wipe the floor with the UWFi troupe. In order to make the company look competitive though, Choshu did protect Takada, giving him a run with the IWGP title. Takada beat Keiji Muto for the belt on the January 4 1996 show to huge heat, on a card with an NJPW vs UWFi theme. It was the only UWFi victory on a show that also featured young talents from both sides square off in a six man tag (notable team members were Yuji Nagata for NJPW and Sakuraba as his opposite number), Riki Choshu defeat Masahito Kakihara in a hard hitting bout, and Shinya Hashimoto beat Kazuo Yamazaki to a big reception.

It wasn't necessarily a career suicide for the UWFi stars or their style. Yamazaki for instance, would sign with NJPW on a full time basis after the invasion angle, and would be a solid player up to the year 2000, tagging with Kensuke Sasaki and winning the IWGP Tag belts on one occasion.

Meanwhile one could definitely make the case that the high attention the UWFi angle received gave credence to a different presentation of the in-ring action. More plainly presented, no-nonsense stars would come to be in vogue.

Koji Kanemoto and Shinjiro Otani in the junior division seemed like throwbacks in a way. Kanemoto in 1992 filled the role of Tiger Mask after All Japan relinquished the rights to the character back to NJPW. He was ultimately never comfortable in performing the role however, and after losing a mask versus mask match to Jushin Liger on January 4 1994, returned to the black tights and boots of a Young Lion. Kanemoto and Liger would wrestle again at the Tokyo Dome two years later and the difference in performance was evident from Kanemoto, suddenly a comfortable performer with a mix of high flying and submission work (Kanemoto would be credited with popularizing the ankle lock, particularly with a grapevined leg, before Ken Shamrock and Kurt Angle favored the hold in the West).

They stood out in a division that had wildman Sabu as its champion briefly in 1995 as well as WAR's Ultimo Dragon, and Black Tiger, portrayed memorably by Eddie Guerrero and less so by Silver King. Where the Junior division had typically been a place to market NJPW to younger fans in the '80s and '90s, Kanemoto, with his hard strikes and submissions, or Otani's similarly stiff looking 'facewash' corner kicks, grounded the division somewhat and earned the attention of purists.

Of course, if you were UWFi through and through, the chances are you were losing for the most part in 1995 and '96, unless your last name was Takada. The defeat of UWFi main card talent only seemed to highlight the significance of Takada winning the IWGP title, that match with Muto bringing basic psychology (Takada working over Muto's arm, Muto Takada's leg) and some hard strikes, ending with the crowd exploding as Muto submitted to a cross armbar (often referenced by the hold's Japanese name, the *juji-gatame* is a reference to the fact that both combatants' bodies are arranged in the shape of the kanji for 'ten' when in the hold). Hashimoto would win the belt back for New Japan three months later in the same building with a similarly heated crowd, but at this point the angle had lost its drive. UWFi would work another cross-promotional angle with WAR before both companies faded away. Still, it was another bright, briefly burning invasion that had an influential fan.

WCW President Eric Bischoff was one of the 54,000 announced attendees at the January Wrestle War show and was impressed with the fervor surrounding the card. Enamoured with the idea of an invading faction battling for the future of the company, he returned to the U.S. and pitched his own take on the concept.

The New World Order would become the stable that propelled WCW to huge success in the States. While it would be overexploited to the point of doing more harm than good to the company in the long run, the cool black-clad heel faction was huge through 1996 and '97.

The knock on effect, then, was an invasion angle in New Japan influencing a faction in the US... Which was then ported back to New Japan. Masahiro Chono was, as we've seen, a major player in the early part of the decade, but really found fame when undergoing a transformation to a black leather clad yakuza gang boss style look. Together with the veteran Masa Saito and Hiroyoshi Tenzan, whose flat top and mullet combo hair style and brusque manner made him seem like a *Fist of the North Star* style anime villain, Chono created the oxymoronic Team Lone Wolf. The ChoTen combination won the IWGP Tag belts on July 16 1996 from Takashi Iizuka and the now NJPW employed Kazuo Yamazaki.

That same summer, Choshu would win the G1 Climax by withstanding Chono's STF hold and beating Mr. August as part of his final big run as a singles star in NJPW. While Choshu had the fairy tale story of a man admittedly past his prime struggling to prove his worth once more, it also presented the drive for Chono to develop yet more of a heel character. He would join the nWo in WCW's continuity at the end of the year, and, in the NJPW universe, would form nWo Japan.

The faction operated in Japan in much the same way as it did in the US, gradually filling out its roster to the point of getting too big for some, and ganging up to beat down their opponents. It would allow a comfortable storyline home for the likes of Kevin Nash and Scott Hall when brought over, and gave WCW prospects like Jeff Farmer a stable to work multiple man tag matches in Japan while waiting for creative direction Stateside (a veteran bit-part player, Farmer would portray a fake heel version of Steve Borden's Sting character in what would ultimately be the highlight of his career).

nWo Japan would grow from Chono, Saito and Tenzan to include 17 members at it's peak. *Photo: Nikkan Sports/AFLO*

nWo Japan, like its American counterpart was a hot merchandise seller, although as with Liger and Tiger Mask merchandise, licensing fees had to be paid back to WCW. Driving the popularity of the group further was a 'will he/ won't he' storyline surrounding Keiji Muto possibly joining the nWo through '97. Helping the mystique of the Muta character was a feud with Jushin Liger in 1996, Liger returning to the ring after surgery to remove a brain tumor, and in the process of becoming a more mat oriented wrestler to conserve his body. In one match, Muta tore at Liger's mask to reveal the painted Kishin Liger, a darker, brutal alter-ego that Liger would come back to on occasion.

Muto and Chono had a new dimension to their rivalry added by the nWo situation, and Muto worked in his Great Muta persona. In May 1997, Muto teamed with the Steiners against the nWo unit of Kevin Nash, Scott Hall and Chono (while for absolutely zero reason, Eric Bischoff provided sporadic English colour commentary to the confused Japanese television audience). In June, The Great Muta teamed with Chono to take on Choshu and Hashimoto. By the end of 1997, Muto 'turned' to join his alter ego in the nWo 'full time' so to speak. As goofy as it sounded, live audiences ate the angle up, a testament to Muto as a performer, who could lean on the mysticism of his twin personae to cover for nagging injuries that were piling up, and change his Muto look to grow a fuller beard, and eventually shave his head as genetics removed his hair.

Siding against the nWo was a mix of veterans and younger talent. Tatsumi Fujinami, now, along with Kengo Kimura, having one last major run in-ring before working more behind the scenes, formed the team that took the tag titles from ChoTen on the 1997 January 4 show for a brief nostalgia run. Choshu, meanwhile, would team with each of his favoured stars through the mid 90s - Nagata, Hashimoto and Sasaki.

The Nagata relationship was brief, as the younger star would head to WCW for a year's excursion in '97. Hashimoto, for his part, was largely above the nWo mix, occasionally tagging against nWo combinations like Muta and Chono, but as a distraction during his massive 489 day title run.

Sasaki was Choshu's pet project though. Having broken away from the Power Warrior character, Sasaki was now a hard headed gruff talking younger version of Choshu himself. After toiling in the upper mid card for the better part of the decade, he would have the proverbial rocket strapped to him in 1997. In the space of one month, he won the G1 Climax over Tenzan, the IWGP Tag titles with Yamazaki, and ended Hashimoto's historic reign, going on to beat Chono and Muto in successive defences.

The peak of the nWo Japan era was Chono winning the IWGP title in August 1998, beating Fujinami with an STF to end The Dragon's final reign in the Osaka Dome. It was a short-lived run though. Chono had been suffering from the accumulation of neck issues, starting with being dropped on his head in his NWA title match with Steve Austin. Mere weeks into his title run, Chono left to recover, and from here nWo Japan's days were numbered.

Muto took over as the *de facto* leader of the group, and while Chono worked a slower pace that worked with his slimy look to make him a heelish character, it was hard to dislike Muto/Muta, balding and beard or no. As a stable of babyfaces, or at least heels the audience had too much respect and admiration for to boo, there was little draw to the nWo concept. The group persisted through 1999 though, with largely good knock on effects. Muto brought Satoshi Kojima into the group, allowing him to team with once rival and dojo classmate Tenzan. The two personalities meshed wonderfully, and TenKojy were an instant favourite tag team, while both were coming into their own as singles talents, too.

Kojima teaming with Tenzan freed up the former's Bull Powers partner and another Choshu pet project, Manabu Nakanishi. A giant man, Nakanishi had a lack of agility working against him even before a litany of injuries that plagued him in the next millennium, but as a brute with bear like swiping forearms, he was popular. He'd be elevated to main event level by the end of the 90's, and beat Muto to win the 1999 G1 Climax. With Nagata returning to Japan working against Tenzan and establishing himself as a charismatic figure with a hard-hitting edge, NJPW was attempting to set a decent foundation for the year 2000 in the wake of nWo's eventual demise.

WCW and UWFi weren't the only two promotions with invading factions in late '90s NJPW, meanwhile. In fact, cross promotion and invasion would almost reach the point of overkill by the end of the decade.

Dai Nihon (Big Japan) Wrestling was formed in 1995 by former All Japan talents Shinya Kojika and Kazuo Sakarada (best known as Kendo Nagasaki, but not the one familiar to British fans, who was portrayed by the distinctly non Japanese Peter Thornley of Stoke). With FMW and IWA Japan in the ascendancy, the pair aimed to hop on the death match wrestling bandwagon, and would eventually manage to create a longer lasting company than either competitor, celebrating twenty years as a promotion in 2015.

In 1997 the company was seeking extra promotion though, and did so by working with NJPW, the extra exposure being traded for losses by most of their talent through '97, mainly on that year's January 4 Dome show. The four inter-promotional matches on that card were clashes of styles at best and disasters at worst; witness Masa Saito against the first of only two people to work a featured January 4 match in shirt and dress shoes, the Great Kojiki, in an abysmal affair (in 2013, Lowki did a much better job of carrying off business wear with ring work). One definite highlight though, was Shinjiro Otani's bout with Yoshihiro Tajiri. BJW adopted FMW and ECW's philosophy of merging hardcore 'garbage' wrestling with more straightforward technical matches throughout their history, and Tajiri represented the latter group. He was the promotion's first junior heavyweight champion, and about to have a successful run in the US spanning ECW and the WWF.

The pair's high impact striking styles gelled well, and it was an enjoyable match if brief at under ten minutes. It was certainly the best junior heavyweight match that card, as it competed with Chris Jericho debuting the Super Liger character (an all silver Black Tiger like counterpart to Liger) against Kanemoto in an infamous stinker. Kanemoto would recover into a great feud with El Samurai, their 1998 Best of the Super Junior final being a classic encounter. 'Super' Jericho never did get the big feud with the original Liger he was hoping for, meanwhile.

The Big Japan interpromotional feud, and folding of FMW and IWA Japan that lead to numerous freelancers looking for work, did see NJPW experiment with hardcore wrestling and gimmick bouts that they had shunned for years. Atsushi Onita himself appeared in the promotion in 1999, feuding with Muta under the guise of the Great Nita, a goofy face painted alter ego with none of the understanding behind what made Muta great. While Muto used his explosive pace to act mysterious and almost snake like, the Great Nita attempted to project a creepy aura by spinning on the spot, arms outstretched like a child trying to make themselves dizzy. The resulting barbed wire exploding ring match was atonal and bizarre in the context of a New Japan show, and the hardcore experiment didn't last.

Spurred on by the UWFi program, NJPW's love affair with MMA would continue into the 2000s to the product's detriment, but for now was used to set up some big drawing matches. After nearly two decades on the outs, Inoki and Satoru Sayama worked together in 1997 and 1998 on an MMA project called the Universal Fighting Arts Organisation, or UFO. After prior attempts to make mixed martial arts into a Japanese phenomenon stalled for Inoki, Pancrase and kickboxing oriented K-1 made a case for MMA in the country, and Inoki wanted to make stars that would span MMA and pro wrestling. Ken Shamrock was in Inoki's sights in early '97 before being courted by WWF, and instead, Inoki sought to build both companies around 1992 Olympic silver medallist judoka Naoya Ogawa. While fighting with UFO, Ogawa also feuded with Muto and Hashimoto in 1997 and '98, before being a part of PRIDE Fighting Championships and its sister wrestling promotion Hustle in the early 2000s.

Ogawa had a shaky start in pro wrestling. His green nature was largely covered up with smoke and mirrors early on, but he still seemed awkward. Not helping were the clashes of styles with opponents he had, such as in August '97 against Muta. Here, Inoki acted as special referee, taking a misting from Muta. There was an angle where Sayama (as manager Tiger King) threw in the towel against Ogawa's will, the whole affair was finished in under ten minutes, and the bout was *still* a mess. However, by working a featured program with Hashimoto whom he had more chemistry with (albeit after a first bout between the two saw Ogawa deliberately try to wear out and expose Hashimoto's lack of 'real combat' credentials), Ogawa managed to gain competency as a pro wrestler as well as a fighter.

Ogawa all but humiliated Hashimoto legitimately in their first match together. Later bouts saw them gel more easily *Photo: Moritsuna Kimura/AFLO*

Ogawa was set to have the biggest match of his career in April of 1998; the plan was for him to face Inoki in his final match. Instead, and somewhat confusingly, a legitimate MMA tournament was set up with the winner getting to participate in the worked match with Inoki. Rather than the chosen Ogawa, the tournament was won by UFC alum and former NWA champion (as the alliance, now a shell of its former self, continued an on again off again relationship with NJPW) Don Frye. Inoki's final match, announced on the January 4 1998 Dome show, was set for April 4 the same year.

Inoki had perhaps one of the longest retirement tours of all time, with the Final Countdown series stretching all the way back to 1995. It had been a three year vanity tour for Inoki to get wins over his favourite opponents, and get significant victories back over stars like Vader. In truth, Inoki had planned to honour tradition in his final bout by losing his last match, but was convinced otherwise, and beat Frye with a Cobra Twist in a mere four minutes (Inoki had his ribs broken early in the bout, hence the brevity).

The April 4 show drew NJPW's biggest gate in history, the equivalent of 7 million USD which has only been beaten by three cards worldwide since. It was also the biggest in a slew of retirements, semi-retirements and deaths that shook Japanese wrestling to its core. On the same January 4 show that the Inoki retirement was announced, Choshu wrestled his last matches, at least for the time being. Not to be outdone by Inoki in the ego stakes, he faced five opponents on the same card, including a significant loss to Takashi Iizuka in a failed bid to make a mega star of him, and a final victory over Liger.

Fujinami would also finish up for the most part in 1998, having his fourth and final run with the IWGP title start on Inoki's last card with a win over Sasaki, before dropping the title to Chono in the summer. He would be named president of the company in 1999, and have to steer the ship through its most difficult years, and a rocky creative partnership with Choshu.

Then, on January 31 1999, Shohei Baba died of cancer. All Japan had seen its peak drawing years go by, but was still prominent in the Japanese wrestling scene. While Mitsuharu Misawa inherited the position of president within the company, there were ruptions between him and Shohei's wife Motoko, who was, to say the least, a divisive figure. Making a power play to seize control of the company, she would organize a board vote to remove Misawa as president. The former Tiger Mask left All Japan, never to return, and on June 16, 2000 took an incredible 24 of the 26 regularly contracted All Japan wrestlers with him to form a new company, NOAH. Only Toshiaki Kawada and Masa Fuchi remained in the company, along with sole foreign talent Maunakea Mossman, who wrestled under the name Taiyo Kea. AJPW, desperate, announced a quick alliance with New Japan in short order, ostensibly to 'break down walls' between the two companies, but in reality to give All Japan some, any, talent to book.

NOAH not only pillaged All Japan's roster, but also its TV time slot with NTV, who reneged on their television deal despite still owning a 15 percent stake in the company. That timeslot by now, once a prime time draw, was a half hour highlight show airing at midnight, with occasional specials. Just as at the turn of the 1990's the rising tide helped all ships, by the turn of the millennium, the increasing drought was leading to beached whales. New Japan's timeslot, too, was steadily pre-empted and tumbled in the schedules before landing in a late night half hour spot. While NOAH would kick off with undeniably high interest meanwhile, there was a growing sense that the market, unable to really support even two big companies at the end of the 1990s, was growing flooded, and all this as Japan's economic bubble was popping; truly the age of flowing cash resulting in big houses for vanity project promotions was long gone.

In October of 1999, a pair of promising talents made their debuts in NJPW. High school amateur Katsuyori Shibata entered the dojo system shortly before his classmate Hiroki Goto would. Hiroshi Tanahashi had trained in New Japan's dojo after a lifelong fandom saw him seek a different path, wrestling in a university student pro wrestling circle along with Masaki Sumitani, who would become a breakout TV star in the mid 2000s as questionable sexual stereotype comedy character Hard Gay (student pro wrestling circles are looked down on by many in the Japanese wrestling scene, seen as glorified backyard wrestling troupes, but have an air of professionalism to them unseen in the West, with an annual super card in Korakuen Hall, and many of their performers transitioning to careers in the Japanese independent circuit). Joining Shinya Makabe, who was toiling in preliminary matches before making a change in his ring name to the now familiar Togi, they would rise to prominence over the next few years, but entered into a tumultuous era that was almost fatal to the company.

The 10 Most Significant Junior Heavyweights in NJPW History

New Japan has had a dedicated junior heavyweight division since 1978, relationships with the WWWF allowing for the creation of a junior heavyweight championship in New York all but designed to be a vehicle for the young, popular, but small Tatsumi Fujinami. From there, the group of smaller stars on the New Japan roster has had their fortunes wax and wane, and their position within the company grow and shrink in significance.

Today, the division is fairly slim, often relying on imports from outside the company such as Bobby Fish and Kyle O'Reilly of Ring of Honor's ReDragon tag team to bulk up a roster that has fairly few mainstays. Of those, the quality of performers is high, (Yujiro) Kushida and regular tag partner, Detroit's Alex Shelley being strong talents on their own or together, but are rarely allowed to shine in long form matches outside of the annual Best of the Super Juniors tournament. In recent years, the junior division has also carried the aura of being a proving ground for stars like Dramatic Dream Team imports Kota Ibushi and Kenny Omega to be given the occasional featured match on a show before moving up to compete with heavyweights. As a result, the now IWGP Junior Heavyweight championship, and certainly its tag team counterpart seem like minor titles in comparison to the Intercontinental and Heavyweight prizes.

This wasn't always the case, and the junior division has carried a much greater significance in the past. In the early 1980s it was a crucial part of New Japan growing its audience in a bid to reach younger viewers. Ultraman perhaps didn't connect, but Tiger Mask did, as did his foes in Marc Rocco as Black Tiger, Dynamite Kid, The Cobra, and the villainous Kuniaki Kobayashi.

Later in the decade, kids drawn in by Tiger Mask's superhero like nature were given the slightly more mature Jushin Liger, and a youth oriented division built around the new IWGP Junior Heavyweight championship. Inaugural champion Shiro Koshinaka had been informed by learning excursions to Mexico, adopting cartwheel dives onto opponents on the floor, and his trademark 'hip attack', hitting opponents with his backside in a move later adopted by current junior star Ryusuke Taguchi.

Koshinaka would tag with heavyweight Keiji Muto, winning the IWGP Tag Team championship to become a double champion, before losing his junior title to Hiroshi Hase, another fiery young star. Both would become upper mid card mainstays in the heavyweight division into the 1990s, Hase having legendary matches with Muto, and Koshinaka teaming with Kobayashi before joining All Japan alum Genichiro Tenryu to form the *Heisei Ishingun* redux of Riki Choshu's original promotion hopping stable. Meanwhile Jushin Liger, Chris 'Pegasus Kid/Wild Pegasus' Benoit, an imported Owen Hart and more would thrill audiences and particularly appeal to teens who were the target of NJPW's mid Saturday afternoon TV slot.

Through the 1990s, NJPW's junior division was a key unique selling point, and what helped the company distinguish itself from strong competition in All Japan, and a host of smaller promotions. As the kids and teens grew older in the middle of the decade, and NJPW wrestlers found themselves embroiled in a cross promotional feud with stars from UWFi, Koji Kanemoto and Shinjiro Otani would rise to prominence as no-nonsense warriors with colourful costumes and eccentric mannerisms taken away. Their feuds with Liger, Benoit, El Samurai and more that they deemed relics of a cartoonish era brought some of the finest in-ring work anywhere in the world in the latter part of the 1990s.

In the 2000s, the division began to wane. Under Riki Choshu's book, the division was de-emphasised with its stars, including Liger and Otani moving to heavyweight in poor runs. Stars were few, and those remaining in the junior division had to work harder to protect their spot on the card. The division has not truly recovered since, but shining stars have been present and have shown hope that the junior heavyweights can once again come to the forefront.

Here, in no particular order, are the ten individuals who carried the most significance in NJPW's junior heavyweight history.

Satoru Sayama

Satoru Sayama seems in retrospect an unusual figure to portray an enduringly popular character that introduced a younger generation to professional wrestling. A devotee of Gotch, Robinson and Kotetsu Yamamoto, he started his career as a Young Lion that used hard kicks and grapples in an extremely self-serious persona. After leaving NJPW amid the scandals that plagued the company in the mid 1980s, he was publicly critical of the showbusiness nature of New Japan. He derided the company as offering fake combat, and sought in UWF to create a promotion more legitimate, and while still pre-determined, much harder hitting.

As a trainer to Naoya Ogawa, Kazuyuki Fujita and more, he was fierce to the point of dangerous sadism, brutally beating prospects with a kendo stick as a motivator. Yet under the Tiger Mask character in the early 1980s, he would become a role model, appearing in some high camp faux documentaries produced by NJPW that highlighted the significance of his hard work and training interspersed with high fiving young children, in the sort of presentation WWF would adopt with Hulk Hogan in the US.

There was every reason for Sayama to be skeptical when approached with the Tiger Mask gimmick in 1981 after returning from the UK having worked under the ridiculous character of Sammy Lee, Bruce's long lost cousin. Yet he was an immense success, and while he would later grow a distaste for less realistic interpretations of pro wrestling, he was able to effortlessly blend the more legitimate with the flashy and high flying. His debut opposite Dynamite Kid would showcase the learning Sayama had undertaken in Europe, and their subsequent feud produced a string of classics.

If wrestling Dynamite, or Marc Rocco as Black Tiger, produced matches of a more European bent, Sayama showed flexibility in working with Hiroaki

'Gran' Hamada, a fellow early NJPW dojo graduate who had been almost literally belittled by management (due to his small stature they labelled him 'Little Hamada'). It was only on his excursion to Mexico that Central American audiences fell in love with him, changing his name to Gran. With Tiger Mask, he produced a series of fantastic bouts that highlighted both men's ability to show acrobatic flair, working intricate sequences of rope running and counter holds, ending with simultaneous dropkicks that as a sequence feels cliched today, but drew entranced screams from audiences more than three decades prior.

As Hamada helped to shape the junior heavyweight style in Japan elsewhere, including the influential Michinoku Pro promotion, Sayama would leave New Japan after a mere three years under the character that defined his career, going on to have a strange relationship with the profession that brought him stardom and the character that made him famous. His significance and popularity during his peak though shaped an entire division, and a host of people's perception of what professional wrestling is.

Tatsumi Fujinami

There are precious few people that were with New Japan at its inception with Inoki, and stayed loyal to the company even longer than its founder did. Kotetsu Yamamoto, who remained as a trainer and official until his 2010 passing, was one. Tatsumi Fujinami is another, and was more involved in different aspects of the company from trainee through to president than arguably anyone else.

It's his seminal run as a junior heavyweight that is of relevance here though. As a teenager joining mentor Inoki in leaving JWA, his talent was obvious and loyalty appreciated, but his size and age precluded him from being a main event star in the 1970s. Hisashi Shinma's position as liaison between New Japan and WWF was what secured the latter's junior heavyweight championship, a title that served as Fujinami's reward, vehicle to superstardom, and origin for the entire division.

Were it not for a two day reign by Ryuma Go (a fellow young prodigy, Go had made his pro debut at age 14 before working in the US, Mexico and Canada), Fujinami would have been WWF Junior Heavyweight champion for 1406 days straight. For more than five years, opposite Go, Chavo Guerrero, later tag team partner Kengo Kimura, and toward the end of his reign the newly hooded Sayama as Tiger Mask, Fujinami introduced and showcased a different style of wrestling. His explosive nature and innovative range of maneuvers, from Dragon Screw leg whips to suplexes and sleepers would become staples in acts of his disciples, including Keiji Muto and Hiroshi Tanahashi, but at the time they were novel and thrilling.

A fresh face with a fresh approach to his craft, it's not hard to see why people took to Fujinami and how 'Dragon Fever' took root. Much like his aforementioned devotees, Fujinami had an uncanny knack for adapting himself to a variety of opponents, equally capable of going hold for hold with Kimura, or allowing Dynamite Kid in their 1980 series to dominate for the majority of the match, sneaking out a surprise intricate pin for a huge reaction.

While his 1982 transition to the heavyweight division and subsequent legendary feud with Riki Choshu would be where Fujinami's career really hit the stratosphere, the formative decade he spent as a smaller competitor cannot be discounted. Fujinami is a pioneer and a standard bearer for a weight class and a generation.

Jushin Thunder Liger

Jushin Liger is one of the most enduring, recognisable and significant characters not only in Japanese junior heavyweight wrestling, but pro wrestling at large regardless of nationality or weight class. Keiichi Yamada, by extension, is one of the medium's most respected figures, a guiding light to dojo trainees and a person that works to elevate younger talent in the latter stages of his career. Today he has a reputation of being what western promoters would call a 'locker room leader'. Much like the most famous of western locker room leaders, who made a decades long legacy out of the ridiculous on paper Undertaker character, Liger could just as easily have been laughed out of the Tokyo Dome on his debut in 1989.

Yet Yamada's ability was able to shine through the layers of afternoon anime camp (the Jushin Liger anime didn't even have any connections to pro wrestling, which eventually helped Yamada to make a clean break with the character, but also made his original appearance feel as shoehorned into the show as Robocop appearing in WCW to help Sting). To younger fans, he was colourful and enigmatic, and to older fans he was incredibly athletic, merging high flying (Yamada popularised the use of the Shooting Star Press) with more power moves that showed off strength made less visible by the trademark bodysuit.

Domestically he would be at the head of the junior heavyweight division through most of the 1990s, producing sterling efforts with the colourful characters that populated the division at the time. From within New Japan, he worked extensively with Akira Nogami, a consistent if underrated figure with a face painted AKIRA persona inspired by *Kabuki* theatre. When the Tiger Mask character returned to NJPW control, he'd wrestle Koji Kanemoto under that hood, leading up to a mask versus mask match at the Tokyo Dome on January 4 1994. The bout was as well remembered for the entrances leading up to it than the action itself or Kanemoto's unmasking. An actor clad in Kanemoto's ring gear leapt from the top of the building onto a crash mat, while a Liger double danced on top of a giant screen before the real thing made his appearance.

The outside talent appearing for NJPW that Liger wrestled were for the most part similarly extravagantly presented. They ranged from Yoshihiro Asai, who shared a lucha influence learned in Mexico and wrestled as the colourful Ultimo Dragon in WAR, to FMW's high flying masked star Eiji 'Hayabusa' Ezaki and Michinoku Pro founder Masanori Murakawa, who wrestled as the ninja master Great Sasuke.

Yet Liger was no mere character player. in-ring, he brought the best performances out of wrestlers of any standard. All the above imports were highly respected in their own rights, and knew that in an interpromotional situation they would invariably have a great match with Liger, and win or lose, come out all the better as individuals and representatives for their company. It's that level of trust that helped make the Super J Cup tournament in 1994 a possibility; the show that made an international superstar out of Sasuke, and presented arguably the best match of either man's career.

Internationally, Liger was an ambassador for NJPW to the globe, mostly with WCW while the two companies had their working arrangement. Most famously with Brian Pillman, Liger was often counted on to set a high standard and invest the crowd in the opening match on many a WCW show, including the very first edition of the promotion's Monday Nitro.

Yamada has played the Liger role for more than a quarter of a century at this point, and his longevity has seen him hold the IWGP Junior Heavyweight championship a record eleven times (his nearest competitor is the fourth Tiger Mask, Yoshihiro Yamazaki, with a mere six). Yamada's adaptability as a worker is of huge significance in this regard, and while many with the high flying style he presented would burn out and be hobbled with mounting injuries, Liger was smart to change his ring style after surgery on a brain tumour in 1996. A silver lining to the potentially lethal cloud that presented was improved chemistry with Kanemoto and Shinjiro Otani, who were building a legacy on running counter to the cartoonish characters the division featured earlier in the decade.

Liger's heel turn and heavyweight run was ill advised, but in transitioning through CTU, Yamada's popularity endured. *Photo Yukio Hiraku/AFLO*

Liger's longevity outlasted brain surgery, the collapse of the company he was most famous in the west for working in, and even an MMA career and being forced to wrestle as a heavyweight. While Liger suffered in the early 2000s under Choshu and Inoki's creative direction, afterward, as leader of CTU, he began to morph into the figure he is now, a support act dedicated to getting the stars of tomorrow, which at that point included Hiroki Goto and Prince Devitt, to the forefront. While this list isn't ranked, it's hard to imagine a numbered list of significant junior heavyweights anywhere from any era, and not have Liger at the top.

Shinjiro Otani

In a period where the bright colourful masked characters of Liger, El Samurai, Ultimo Dragon and Great Sasuke ruled the roost, Shinjiro Otani was a breath of fresh air. Having made his debut in 1992 at the age of twenty, Otani had the typical path of a Young Lion, working preliminary matches and undergoing learning excursions in Mexico.

Unlike many of his contemporaries however, Otani never shunned the traditional black tights and boots in favour of a superhero character on his return. Sensing a sea change in the mid 1990s with a focus on a more realistic style, with NJPW engaged in a hot feud with UWFi, Otani brought a no-nonsense persona with a grounded style that made things even more exciting when he did take to the air.

Like on again, off again partner and rival Koji Kanemoto, Otani would have phenomenal chemistry with the colourful personae that he presented himself as the antithesis of. Otani put in tremendous Tokyo Dome performances against El Samurai and Ultimo Dragon in particular, while working as a team with Kanemoto, would engage in feuds with Liger and imports like Dr. Wagner Jr as the 1990s wore on. The result was that Otani was a leading part of the shoot style zeitgeist before things were taken too far down the vale tudo route in the early 2000s.

Against top UWFi junior star Kazushi Sakuraba, Otani worked similarly well. Their June 17 1996 match was spectacular and showcased Otani's tremendous ring psychology; while the audience expected a striking and submission style, and that was what the two presented, the match began and ended with flair, Sakuraba exploding out the gate with a German suplex to Otani, and the match ending with an Otani springboard dropkick, and a Dragon suplex with a transition to rear naked choke rather than a bridging pin. It was the hybrid of MMA and pro-style wrestling that so few in the ensuing years would pull off convincingly.

Otani was only once IWGP Junior Heavyweight champion, but his reign was made more significant by also being the final J-Crown champion. Yet another concept brought about by Liger's influence, the title, active for just over a year starting in the summer of 1996, was a unification of seven junior heavyweight titles from around the world, including the Mexican UWA belt Otani held through much of 1995 and 1996, a pair of junior heavyweight titles recognised by the NWA, and the WWF Light Heavyweight championship. Ultimately NJPW surrendered all but the IWGP Junior Heavyweight championship in November 1997 after the WWF requested their title back, planning to have a focus on their light heavyweight division on a regular TV basis.

Otani is more than just an answer to a trivia question though. While his transition to heavyweight under much duress at Choshu's behest in 2001 did not pan out, and saw him depart the company for Zero One, his junior run was fresh and dynamic, and his in-ring performances almost flawless.

Koji Kanemoto

While Otani never portrayed anyone other than himself after finishing his Young Lion years, Koji Kanemoto initially did have a gimmick assigned to him. Not just any gimmick either; he would be the third incarnation of Tiger Mask, a character portrayed so famously by Sayama, and Mitsuharu Misawa, the latter relinquishing the mask with considerable relief at not having the pressure of living up to a fictional character's reputation.

Kanemoto's run with the mask was brief, less than two years in fact. These were big shoes to fill, and while the young former judoka tried valiantly to do so, he struggled. On being unmasked by Liger though, Kanemoto managed to find his voice as a performer.

Much like Otani, he would use the Tiger Mask run as motivation to strip away extraneous facets of his act, become more sparing with the flashier moves of his former self (with the knock on benefit of helping reduce the toll on his body) and have a similar kayfabed distaste for the colourful characters that surrounded the pair in the division.

His mat based delivery made use of his legitimate training, merging grappling and submissions (Kanemoto made the ankle lock a popular wrestling hold, while his Koji Clutch is often imitated) with hard strikes ('face washing' a seated opponent with a boot in the corner was similarly a Kanemoto original that was adapted by many, Otani included) and the ability to go up for a moonsault when he needed to.

As with Otani, Kanemoto's different approach lead to exciting in-ring clashes of styles. Against El Samurai, with whom he had a lasting rivalry, or when facing Jushin Liger in one of their four separate January 4th meetings (only the last of which in 2000, a sub five minute angle designed to help establish Liger's unfortunate Black Liger heel turn and progression to heavyweight) was where Kanemoto really shone, though he, alongside Minoru Tanaka, was also a highlight in the early days of the largely forgettable IWGP Junior Tag scene. Unlike Otani, Kanemoto, thanks to being paired with Tanaka at the time before being injured, was never forced into heavyweight competition at the turn of the millennium, but instead had heavyweight singles matches occur more organically.

He would enter into the G1 Climax in 2004 and 2006, with a semi-final performance in the second attempt leading to challenging Hiroshi Tanahashi for the IWGP Championship while still a junior in September 2006 and again in February 2007.

Arguably the finest performer in the world when at his peak, Kanemoto inspired fans and fellow wrestlers alike, and was rewarded with IWGP Junior title reigns lasting nearly three years in total, and a trio of Best of the Super Junior victories.

Prince Devitt

The LA Dojo might not have been the most cost effective side project for a cash strapped NJPW at the time, but while active it saw some of the best talent of their generation through its doors. Devitt is a significant graduate of a system that also housed Samoa Joe, Bryan Danielson and more, and while those other two never had long runs in New Japan, Devitt's contributions made him the undeniable ace of a division that was fading from the company limelight.

While working with Ryusuke Taguchi as fun loving tag team Apollo 55 saw some fine performances, it was as a singles performer that Devitt shone. A high flier, but with a vicious bent, he had the no-nonsense look of Kanemoto and Otani and the easy charisma of the characters that preceded them. Much like Brooklyn import Lowki, who had several brief runs in the company throughout the 2000s, Devitt had some brutal kicks and double foot stomps. His crisp mat work evoked Chris Benoit, a comparison New Japan themselves dabbled with by briefly putting him under a mask as Pegasus Kid 2 early on in his career. His Bloody Sunday finisher, meanwhile almost evoked Hashimoto's DDT.

The hypothetical of had Devitt been in New Japan during the mid 1990s heyday of the junior division, throws up all manner of fantasy booking scenarios. As was, when maturing in the division, he would often be working with imports into the company, helping solidify him as a fan favourite who the crowd identified as being a star of their own creation.

His work with DDT stand out Kota Ibushi was electric, a Wrestle Kingdom 6 bout between the two comfortably earning match of the night status. The two had phenomenal chemistry, with Devitt's timing perfect in receipt of Ibushi's intricate hurricanrana and moonsault spots, and the finish, a top rope Bloody Sunday, was scintillating.

That match was months after an injury to guest entrant Naomichi Marufuji saw Devitt entered into the G1 tournament. His impressive performances, including an upset win over Hiroshi Tanahashi, turned heads and suggested a transition to heavyweight down the road.

WWE signed Devitt when he was still in the midst of that transition, creating yet another wave of unrequited New Japan fantasy booking scenarios. The period of change, however, created his best work, and made Devitt the most interesting star anywhere in the wrestling world during 2013. Working with Tanahashi in Korakuen Hall in a New Japan Cup match, the fans, often hardcore and contrarian got behind him, while the ace complied and worked in a heelish manner. Devitt wrestled like someone with a point to prove, gradually bending rules as he shot Tanahashi into chairs here, or held a hold in the ropes there. As the two faced off in subsequent bouts, Devitt steadily came across as more desperate and more eager to seem like he belonged with the heavyweights, by any means necessary.

Devitt and Ibushi would have phenomenal chemistry *Photo: Yukio Hiraku/AFLO*

This would lead to the formation of the Bullet Club soon after, and some of the most electric heel heat seen by anyone in the company for a very long time. The group helped set up Devitt to join the likes of Fujinami as one of few to have significant runs in both junior and heavyweight divisions, before the lure of America cut things short. There are a lot of 'what it's when it comes to Devitt in New Japan, but what he actually achieved makes him an easy addition to this list.

El Samurai

Osamu Matsuda was part of New Japan for over 20 years. He is a former IWGP Junior Heavyweight champion, and was one of the select few to hold the J-Crown. That said, the character of El Samurai isn't quite on the same level as Liger or Tiger Mask when it comes to instantly identifiable juniors to casual fans. Yet while the division was never built around him, his consistent work at or near the top of his field was testament to his ability, and that he never was *the* go-to guy when it came to New Japan juniors is testament to the strength of the division when he was most active.

His ring name evoked his classic Japanese training as part of the New Japan dojo's class of 1986, as well as his learning excursion in Mexico. His ring gear echoed his name, seeing Matsuda don a mask that echoed samurai head-dress, while in matches he combined the Mexican hurricanranas with more solid powerbombs and inverted DDTs.

He was a high level mechanic that worked extremely well with everyone, including Liger, whom he won the IWGP Junior belt from in the autumn of 1992, AKIRA in occasional tag bouts, and Ultimo Dragon.

It was with Kanemoto that El Samurai gelled best with, however. The characters clashed naturally, Kanemoto being someone that rescinded his masked persona and Matsuda embracing it. With both men arguably at their performing peak, they faced off in the 1997 Best of the Super Juniors finals in a tremendous bout. Kanemoto was relentless in working over Samurai's knee, and when the latter had a chance to take over, some nasty stomps to the head, in between selling the bad wheel, provided the receipt for every laid in Kanemoto shot. For every bit Kanemoto was a mean brutal heel, Samurai was able to work as a master salesman, unleashing simple maneuvers to huge impact as every movement seemed to take the wind from his sails.

Kanemoto, ripping at Samurai's mask, landing a huge reverse hurricanrana, and performing a perfect moonsault, made his feats look effortless, with excellent facial expressions radiating disdain. It all made

Samurai's kick outs, and shots of offense more impactful, as he showed the very essence of the fighting spirit the fans craved. A reverse DDT from the top followed by two more in-ring saw the crowd in rapture and El Samurai victorious.

El Samurai was the bride that night while so often being the bridesmaid during his career at large. Yet his body of work spanning three decades speaks for itself, and he is one of the best supporting players in NJPW history.

Minoru Tanaka

Debuting in 1999, Minoru Tanaka entered New Japan as a junior heavyweight as the division was about to face a lot of turbulence. Within a couple of years of his debut, Liger was a black mask clad heavyweight, Otani was also moving up, and the division was being pushed heavily into the background.

In that difficult period though, Tanaka was a figure of stability, doubtless given special consideration on account of his shoot style background. After starting with Battlarts, a work shoot promotion two spin-offs removed from UWFi, Tanaka worked with a few different indies before coming into NJPW. Sharing a mat based approach and usage of leg bars and ankle locks with Kanemoto, he was a natural tag partner for the older star, and the pair would indeed win the IWGP Junior Tag titles together. Tanaka would also wrestle with other young prospects in singles matches through 2000 and 2001, facing off in a series of bouts with Katsuyori Shibata and Shinya Makabe, with whom his explosiveness and Makabe's slugfest approach gelled to strong effect.

In June 2000, Tanaka won his first of four IWGP Junior Heavyweight championships from Tatsuhito Takaiwa. He was growing in popularity as a youthful star in the Kanemoto/ Otani mould but with more of a tendency toward high flying moves augmenting his mat work. Then, with a shrinking and aging audience for the promotion at large, Tanaka was given the kid friendly character of Heat.

Under a brightly coloured mask and a character that cross promoted the *Tokon Heat* videogame (itself by no means a success), the three year run for Tanaka as Heat produced precious few highlights. Relinquishing the gimmick, Tanaka would have his last junior reign, submitting former tag partner Kanemoto with a cross arm breaker on Christmas Eve 2006.

Tanaka's performances either side of a period when the junior division was cast into the wilderness, as well as his work after NJPW in All Japan and currently Wrestle 1 are of an undeniable quality. Heat might be quietly papered over, but Minoru was of rare talent.

Pegasus Kid/Wild Pegasus

Chris Benoit likely headed to the New Japan dojo as a 19 year old with a view to emulate his idol Tom Billington. It's easy to imagine Benoit undergoing the arduous training and living the dojo lifestyle with visions of the Tiger Mask/Dynamite Kid series as inspiration. While Dynamite's time in NJPW was relatively brief, before he headed to All Japan and found fame teaming with Davey Boy Smith, Benoit has a longer legacy with the company.

With Billington's influence on display in his ring style, Benoit liberally borrowing Dynamite's snap suplex and diving headbutt, it's not surprising that NJPW would bill Benoit as the second coming of Dynamite, dubbing him Pegasus Kid.

As Pegasus Kid, Benoit reluctantly worked under a mask for two years, but still turned in impressive performances against domestic stars like Liger (from whom he won his only IWGP Junior Heavyweight championship on August 19 1990) to imports like Steven Regal and Owen Hart, the foreigners able to comfortably work with a fellow English speaker, but the crowds able to invest in the Canadian as a product of the New Japan dojo.

Benoit demasked in late 1991 after a mask versus mask match with Jushin Liger. Tied to Liger for much of his time in Japan, and being a crucial high quality opponent for him as he grew into the role, Benoit was to Yamada as Billington had been to Sayama (as Tiger Mask) in many ways. Now no longer Pegasus Kid, he took on the more driven Wild Pegasus moniker. Benoit came into his own in the mid 1990s, wrestling less like a Dynamite Kid tribute act, and augmenting his style to incorporate mat work with its own feel, and a harder edge closer to the 'Crippler' persona he'd use in the west.

The pinnacle of Benoit's Japanese career was on April 16, 1994. The Super J Cup, organized by Liger, was a one-night tournament featuring 14 of the best junior wrestlers from NJPW, indies and international promotions. As Best of the Super Juniors winner from the prior year, Benoit received a bye into the quarterfinals, but still wrestled three times in matches that held together as one story.

Against the second Black Tiger, (portrayed by Benoit's friend Eddie Guerrero, and with whom Benoit would have several outstanding efforts around the world), Benoit would counter a cross body into an arm drag and quick pin fall. It set Benoit as somewhat of an outsider to win by having him take the bulk of Guerrero's offense in the opening round. No-one believed Gedo would have a chance of winning, but he had enough false finishes in their ten minute semi-final affair to make some question themselves. Great Sasuke meanwhile had wrestled a longer form, hard fought bout with Liger in the semis, and polishing off the junior ace would have had some expecting the outsider would win the whole tournament.

The final was a masterpiece. Sasuke dominated the early going while Benoit sold not being able to have a solution for his acrobatic offense. Control shifted after a Pegasus lariat, and despite Sasuke's stronger propensity for high flying, it would be Benoit with the match's first dive to the floor.

As the pair exchanged momentum, fans were largely in Sasuke's corner, perhaps in deference to his nationality, or more likely due to the star making night he was having. When Sasuke finally landed a quebrada to Benoit, Sumo Hall exploded, and the crowd, already biting on near falls as Benoit evoked Fujinami with a Dragon Suplex earlier, were even more invested. Both indulged in insanely risky spots; Benoit took a suplex from inside the ring to the floor, while Sasuke dropkicked Benoit from the top rope onto concrete outside. In the end, Wild Pegasus would be triumphant after Benoit landed a gut wrench from the top rope, and the Ryogoku crowd had seen a fitting main event to one of the greatest single nights of pro wrestling of all time.

Not long afterward, Western success beckoned for Benoit, who would briefly work with ECW before moving on to WCW. He would have his last New Japan match as Wild Pegasus just before signing with the WWF, working with Hiroyoshi Tenzan on January 4, 2000. Billed as a super heavyweight at this stage, he was even more muscular than he had been years prior, where he had already looked incredibly thick for a junior wrestler.

Benoit's life ended in terrible circumstances, but his in-ring work was a wonder to behold, and his contributions to the junior division outstanding, outstripping even those of his hero.

Kuniaki Kobayashi

As wrestling in Japan was still breaking away from the Japan versus foreigner booking mentality, Japanese heels were rare in the early 1980s. Ones in the junior division even more so; the athleticism of the junior stars shone through and made them hard not to like, and its stars were positive role models, marketed toward kids.

Kuniaki Kobayashi was a rare breed. He did reasonably little in the early years of his career and NJPW's existence, before heading on an excursion to the US and returning with a new attitude. Opposite Tiger Mask he was a wonderful demonic foil, his rule breaking tendencies earning him just as much vitriol as the charismatic Dynamite Kid, who had nationalism to call on. Dozens of times, through 1982 and 1983, Kobayashi would refuse handshakes with Sayama, attack him before the bell, get disqualified as he refused to relinquish holds in the ropes, or in the climax to their feud in June 1983, be distracted for a second to try and reveal Sayama underneath the Tiger Mask, before being rolled up and beaten.

As Sayama moved on from Tiger Mask, Kobayashi made a similarly good fit in Riki Choshu's *Ishingun*, before they left for All Japan as part of the 1984 exodus from the company. Returning just as the IWGP Junior Heavyweight championship was established, he would become the fourth champion in its history, winning the belt in a tournament final after Shiro Koshinaka injured his ankle and was forced to vacate. He would lose the belt soon after to Hiroshi Hase, but his brief reign was a nod to the effort Koshinaka had put in, by now a 14 year veteran at just 31.

Teaming with Koshinaka to form the *Heisei* update of the *Ishingun* team, Kobayashi would work as a heavyweight through the 1990s before retiring at the turn of the millennium. As a 'love to hate' character he was a fresh approach to junior wrestling in his younger years, and as a veteran offered much to generations to come.

9

A Fall From Grace

It was an attempt to keep a struggling company above water, but Masanobu Fuchi walking to the ring in Ryogoku on August 10, 2000 to shake Choshu's hand and ring in an era of cooperation between All and New Japan was a big deal. AJPW had little in the way of talent to bring to the table, obviously, with only Fuchi, Toshiaki Kawada and Taio Kaea under contract, but fresh matches were created with real emotion attached to them.

Chono, who had returned from his neck injury to create a new stable, Team 2000 to first feud with and then absorb nWo Japan, interrupted the moment to jaw at Choshu. Conveniently enough, Choshu had booked his way out of retirement a couple of months prior to work with Atsushi Onita who was, bafflingly, still around. It meant for ready made programs with Chono and Hashimoto as NJPW loyalists; strong angles have at least some element of art imitating life, and there was a sense of the company faithful frustrated at the joining of forces, and at many of Choshu's decisions (influenced by Inoki's increasingly invasive watching brief).

The undisputed highlight of this All/New Japan alliance was the dream matchup between AJPW Triple Crown champion Toshiaki Kawada and IWGP title holder Kensuke Sasaki.

Kawada had finished the 20th century with a famous feud with Mitsuharu Misawa. This included a June 1999 match that saw the All Japan ace break his arm and continue wrestling, in the process accidentally creating the infamous '*ganso* bomb', wherein Kawada didn't have the power to elevate Misawa for a normal powerbomb and instead dropped the former Tiger Mask on the back of his neck.

Sasaki, meanwhile, was in the midst of his second IWGP title reign, having beaten the aging Genichiro Tenryu for the belt. Tenryu in NJPW was part of a last-ditch piece of cross promotion to help his flagging WAR company; WAR would go under in June 2000, though, and most of its talent would bulk up the AJPW roster in the wake of the mass exodus to NOAH.

Sasaki and Kawada were a perfect match for one another. Sasaki was Choshu's chosen one, and a wrestler seemingly created in the former ace's image. Kawada meanwhile put similar emphasis on strikes and projecting a hard man persona.

On October 10 2000, Kawada/Sasaki took place in the Tokyo Dome. 54,000 in attendance and a strong TV special audience saw a phenomenal match, Sasaki playing up his Choshu tutelage throughout with his lariats, mannerisms and use of the Scorpion Death Lock, as announcers played up the handshake a month prior as facilitating the bout.

Kawada and Sasaki were both on painful looking form, the bulls charging each other with lariats in turn, refusing to go down. It's a spot often overused in Japanese wrestling, but was given considerable gravitas due to the people involved, and the sweat that flew with each mighty hit. Eventually Kawada picked up the win, and despite the match being a non-title one, Sasaki refused to receive his IWGP title afterward. He vacated the belt, saying his defeat made him unworthy of it, and this would set up a tournament for January 4 2001.

It was a fantastic piece of storytelling, in-ring as both stars were defending the pride of their company, and out, as Sasaki began a road to redemption. The follow-up tournament was of a high quality too, with Sasaki advancing past Chono and Kawada beating Tenzan on the way to the obvious return match final, this time Sasaki getting his win back. The rematch lacked the drama of the September bout, but was slotted into such a great story that it didn't matter.

The tournament also managed to eclipse Choshu wrestling Hashimoto to a rare non-contest and a negative reaction. Hashimoto, as we touched on previously, had already elevated Naoya Ogawa to main event pro wrestler level with a feud that started out with the legitimate judoka attempting to send a message to Hashimoto, who had banked on perception being reality for his hard man character.

The program had reached its peak in April 2000, with Hashimoto putting his career on the line in a Tokyo Dome match that drew well even with no-one buying into the stipulation. Hashimoto lost, but returned that same summer, wrestling president Tatsumi Fujinami. Hashimoto was supposedly allowed to wrestle on condition he did so in plain black Young Lion garb; he reneged on that stipulation too, and beat Fujinami under his full gimmickry.

Now, with Chono and Team 2000 (including a tag combination with Scott Norton, who had in 1999 become the second foreign IWGP champion) squaring off with Fuchi and other freshly AJPW aligned talent after interrupting the handshake moment in August, it was Hashimoto who was working real discontent with Choshu into a match at the Dome.

In truth, Hashimoto had been fired two months earlier after butting heads with Choshu over the direction of the company. Hashimoto saw the wrestling market becoming overcrowded with a third company in NOAH joining All and New Japan, and indies struggling to get by or going out of business leading to a lot of out of work wrestlers. He proposed starting Zero, which would be a separate promotion working within New Japan. It would be a 'super indie' of sorts, recruiting from all over the country and with a younger focus, giving them a place to work, and giving New Japan a potential talent pool to pluck from whenever they may need it. In modern hindsight, it was a similar idea to WWE's NXT, which has successfully captured an audience that had been turned off by typical wrestling fare on Monday nights, and appropriately enough includes former NJPW talent on its roster.

Choshu hated the idea, and nixed it. Hashimoto persisted though, and was fired in October 2000 for his troubles, leading him to take the Zero name and start Pro Wrestling Zero-One. Ironically, a plan that had been created to help NJPW by consolidating a rapidly flooding market instead added yet another competitor into the shrinking pond.

The Choshu versus Hashimoto match at the Dome was a chance for Zero One to get some publicity, but Choshu refused to lose in a big drawing match, as well he should, arguably. Hashimoto wouldn't do the honours either, understandably enough given a fledgling company image to protect. Instead the two tore into each other with legitimate closed fist punches that may well have been thrown with some malice aforethought. Fujinami stepped in the ring and waved off the match to a chorus of boos. It was the low point in a strong show, and a similar lack of consistent thought and quality affected the company through the early 2000s.

Key people harmed in an era of inconsistent booking included the junior heavyweights. Once what distinguished NJPW from All Japan, Choshu moved to de-emphasize the division by bringing its bigger stars up to heavyweight. Shinjiro Otani and Jushin Liger were both brought up to the heavyweight division, and both felt out of place. Otani, a big deal and popular star in the junior division, was routinely beaten as a heavyweight, including by Sasaki in his sole IWGP title challenge. Frustrated, he left to join Hashimoto in Zero One.

Liger was similarly done a disservice by his stint as a heavyweight in 2000 and 2001. He'd turn heel and switch out his traditional red and white bodysuit and mask to black garb, the black Liger being largely rejected by fans, and not in a 'love to hate' regard. Liger would later receive a change in persona, being given the CTU stable to lead (yes, standing for Counter Terrorism Unit. *24* was an instant hit on Japanese TV, but one has to wonder whether Jack Bauer needed a presence in Japanese wrestling) in what was an enjoyable gimmick. Papering over some of the damage done, it provided a storyline home for Jado and Gedo's transition into gangster like personae, and as allowed young talent like Hiroki Goto and Fergal 'Prince' Devitt to flourish.

Still, the heavyweight diversion did nothing for Liger, and nor did finding himself in a mercifully brief MMA career. On November 30, 2002 Pancrase found itself short an opponent for Minoru Suzuki, who appropriately enough was fighting for the last time in an MMA setting before returning to pro wrestling. Liger, bizarrely, was offered up by New Japan, and subsequently demolished in short order; probably not the smartest course of action in dealing with a talent that had suffered from a brain tumor a handful of years earlier.

Liger was the very tip of the iceberg when it came to careers damaged by ill-advised experiments with MMA. Despite Choshu in the booking role, and Fujinami being listed as the president of the company, this was still the house that Inoki built, had a majority ownership stake in, and felt free to move in and out of at will.

After UFO folded, Inoki's new MMA project was Inoki Bom-Ba-Ye, an annual New Year's Eve show starting in 2000. When Bom Ba Ye 2000 at the Osaka Dome, an event cross promoted between New Japan and PRIDE as the MMA promotion was rapidly growing in momentum, drew an impressive 42,753 people, Inoki's long held dream of displaying New Japan talent as the strongest of all martial artists seemed to have legs. Such thinking was ill advised, to put it mildly; the Osaka show had been a novelty draw, and consisted entirely of worked bouts. The orchestration protected the talent to an extent, though made for a similarly awkward viewing experience as the Real Martial Arts bouts decades earlier.

At least it meant for protected reputations as across the board there was an even enough balance of martial artist and wrestler victories. Kazushi Sakuraba submitted Kendo Kashin, who was one of the few remaining juniors during the Choshu mandated transitions to heavyweight, and the injury to junior ace, Koji Kanemoto. That was redressed by Keiji Muto and Nobuhiko Takada (who was back in pro wrestling for the time being), beating Ken Shamrock and Don Frye. In the main event, meanwhile, a one off exhibition for Inoki, with Renzo Gracie, ended in a draw.

The card should by rights have been a one-off crossover buoyed by curiosity buys. Inoki, though, took the ball and sprinted with it, with an emphasis on what was branded vale tudo. That meant MMA fighters in NJPW and vice versa, worked matches having a mat based grappling style to get around the limitations of newcomers, and wrestlers being absolutely crushed in legitimate fights.

Kazuyuki Fujita, despite being a project NJPW were interested in from 1993 as he was still invested in his amateur career, was a poor fit as IWGP champion, selling offense awkwardly and engaging in grounded bouts that had their place - but not in the main event of every big pro wrestling show. Tadao Yasuda, who had done relatively little in the mid 90s NJPW midcard, suddenly found himself pushed to the moon after a couple of PRIDE fights saw him victorious; again, he wasn't IWGP material. Meanwhile the NJPW dojo, and satellite LA dojo established by Inoki, attempted as much as possible to train hybrid martial artists/wrestlers, including Lyoto Machida, a project who would ultimately leave and go on to super stardom in the UFC.

Yasuda served as the transitional champion for Yuji Nagata, who was finally given the nod after being hugely appreciated by the fan base since his return from WCW in 1998, and was seemingly exactly what Inoki was trying to project. He presented a mix of devastating kicks, the beautiful suplexes he used as a Young Lion, strong grappling skills, and a charisma that seemed to burst through the TV screen. Nearly a decade removed from his debut, Nagata won the 2001 G1 Climax, and then the IWGP championship from Yasuda for a one year reign.

New Japan drew 50,000 plus on January 4 2002 to see Nagata take on Jun Akiyama in a strong, traditional pro wrestling match centered around Nagata working on Akiyama's neck with exploder suplexes and piledrivers (the match was cross promoted with NOAH, which had Akiyama as its GHC champion, and was unquestionably the hottest wrestling product in Japan at the time thanks to phenomenal bouts with Akiyama and the legendary Misawa/Kenta Kobashi rivalry). One year later, it was fewer than 30,000 heading to the Dome (and heavily comped at that) for Nagata defending the IWGP title against another MMA import in Josh Barnett. Barnett would be a valuable influence in the LA dojo, assisting talent to create solid, legitimate seeming work. He was a fighter and not a performer though, and the poor bout that ensued with Nagata was met with near silence.

Conversely, Nagata was a tremendous pro wrestler, and not a high level fighter. This should have been obvious from the outset, yet in December 2001, Nagata was placed into a debacle of a fight for PRIDE with Mirko Cro Cop. He was demolished in 18 seconds after a head kick knocked him out;

this arguably hurt Nagata's drawing potential before getting the belt at all, especially when plans were to defend the IWGP title against fighters who weren't trained for wrestling.

This wasn't the 70s, when audiences didn't really understand what they were seeing in 'real' martial arts matches but for the most part took their legitimacy at face value. Here, worked shoots just looked ridiculous, and nobody bought Nagata as someone who could handle himself in a legitimate fight against a renowned competitor. This didn't stop the dull vale tudo matches coming, or from Nagata being put into yet another fight for PRIDE post IWGP reign, this time with Fedor Emelianenko.

It was a downright irresponsible booking move; Fedor at this point had a 14-1 record, while Nagata was 0-1. Nagata went down in barely a minute, commenting afterward that he wasn't cut out for MMA, but at the same time, could only expect to be put in more matches as long as he was under contract to NJPW. What's all the more galling about the fights that damaged Nagata's standing, and could have harmed his longevity (thankfully, and miraculously, Nagata is still active in 2015 and one of the current NJPW roster's longest serving members) was that NJPW didn't see a single Yen from the curiosity the stunt fights offered; all the money went to PRIDE, while little attention was drawn to the fake fighters who couldn't cut it in the real world in New Japan.

Thankfully, the company started to see sense by 2004, and Nagata would be back on track by the 2004 Wrestle World show on January 4, wrestling Kensuke Sasaki in a brutal and bloody match. His career was on the road to redemption.

In the meantime, Yoshihiro Takayama was given the IWGP title. Takayama was a UWFi alum, who briefly worked for New Japan when the two companies were cooperating, had headed to AJPW in the wake of its folding, and then followed Misawa to NOAH. A tall, imposing figure with a beautiful 'Everest' German suplex, Takayama again fit into the Inoki mould of tough looking guy with an apparently legitimate background, that like Nagata, could go in the ring and produce high quality matches with the right opponents. A more smash-mouth type than Nagata in legitimate and worked environments, Takayama left NOAH in 2002 to pursue the hybrid MMA/NJPW route, and Inoki brought back the old NWF title for him to hold.

The title was intended to be along similar lines as the Real Martial Arts title, or the Greatest 18 club; the toughman belt, which had the same logical issues surrounding it that its predecessors had. If the NWF belt was for legitimately tough competitors, what did that say of the IWGP champion? It wasn't as if NWF title matches were presented as different in any way to the IWGP title bouts; both were filled with challengers outside the world of pro wrestling in dull bouts.

As one example, the semi main event of the Nagata and Barnett card was Takayama against Tsuyoshi Kosaka; a fighter famous for being the '1' in Fedor's 14-1 record when he knocked out Nagata. A snooze that only saw the crowd awaken briefly for Takayama's German, a power outage midway through the bout wasn't even enough to get a reaction from the slim crowd, who possibly were glad the whole affair might be over. The belt was quickly sealed back into the IWGP title when Takayama beat Nagata on May 2 2003, on a strong show if one ignored the five worked shoot matches on it. Also on the card, NOAH's Kenta Kobashi defeated Chono in a hotly anticipated bout.

The show performed much better than in January at the Dome; yet again, though, Takayama and the championship was harmed by a poor MMA record, although Takayama was a more willing participant than Nagata. A humble 0-4 record included losses to Don Frye, and Bob Sapp, the giant former WCW trainee who had become a surprise megastar in Japan in the mid 2000s with marketing deals and TV appearances lessening any damage his fairly poor fighting record would do.

Unlike Nagata, Takayama's longevity was severely compromised by combining pro wrestling and MMA, and despite being the same age as Nagata, was visibly aged by his fighting experience. He lost a great deal of mobility, becoming a legend style special attraction for various wrestling companies after his run with and around the IWGP title ended.

Speaking of Bob Sapp, meanwhile, the incestuous nature of wrestling and MMA saw him too win the IWGP title in March 2004, before vacating the belt barely two months later after (surprise) losing a fight in K1. With dwindling houses, scattershot booking had become the order of the day, long term IWGP title reigns thrown out for throwing champions at the proverbial wall in the hope that one would stick. This would lessen the impact of a pair of notable first IWGP title reigns, one a long time coming, and one coming far too soon.

Bob Sapp was a legitimate celebrity coup, and did have a pro wrestling background having trained with WCW. He didn't move the needle for New Japan though. *Photo: Yukio Hiraku/AFLO*

Hiroyoshi Tenzan had been a consistently reliable workhorse for New Japan for over 12 years when he finally won the title from Takayama on November 3 2003. The TenKojy tag team with Satoshi Kojima produced consistently great matchups from their forming in 1999 until Kojima headed to All Japan during the AJPW/NJPW alliance that saw Kojima seize All Japan's Triple Crown championship. The former nWo Japan members would often find themselves wrestling combinations from Chono's follow-up stable Team 2000, producing strong performances from the combination of Chono and Nakanishi (who had found his stride with a thrilling 60 minute draw with Nagata in a pro wrestling highlight of Nagata's IWGP title defenses). They even worked around the numerous limitations of one Dalip 'Giant' Singh Rana, a huge Indian brought into Team 2000 and paired with Giant Silva before heading to WWE (nee WWF) as the Great Khali (Silva meanwhile would be another New Japan talent to have an unremarkable MMA career).

Tenzan winning the IWGP title was the culmination of a decade plus journey. His match with Takayama was built around this fact, and performed in-ring, but drew poorly at the box office. Yokohama Arena was only half full and heavily comped for a card dominated by worked vale tudo bouts with the last two matches being Takayama and Tenzan, and the beginnings of a long running and tremendous rivalry between Nagata and Minoru Suzuki. Tenzan was cited as the problem with the low box office, not the proven lack of drawing power for the hybrid cards, and his reign only lasted a month.

In place of a wrestler winning his first IWGP title after more than twelve years active was a wrestler winning the title after barely more than one. Shinsuke Nakamura was the youngest IWGP champion in history at just 23 years of age, and the hotshot push to the title for him, befitting of his 'supernova' moniker was definitely attributable to his coming through the Inoki dojo, and being trained in Brazilian jiu jitsu. His natural charisma was hidden behind a buttoned down serious shooter persona with a cross armbar finish a long way removed from the flashy Boma Ye knee he would grow to adopt, and his first two years in the business saw him not only winning the IWGP title, but fighting Daniel Gracie and a pair of middling fighters in Jan Nortje and Alexey Ignashov. Unlike Nagata's MMA run, Nakamura was protected somewhat by the choice of opponents made for him, and he actually ended his fighting career with a positive 2-1 record, even looking competitive with Gracie.

He was too young a champion though, and didn't truly seem comfortable in his role. After a run that saw nagging injuries pile up, particularly after a vicious bout with Takayama in January 2004 at the Dome, Nakamura vacated the belt and on his return worked lower down the card, before embarking on an excursion to Mexico that helped shape the iconic character he would become.

Nakamura was part of a trio of young stars that NJPW was attempting to market as the New Three Musketeers; successors to the Muto, Chono and Hashimoto era. Joining Nakamura was Hiroshi Tanahashi and Katsuyori Shibata, and while all three did make it to the main event scene eventually, the paths they took weren't quite how the company had initially envisioned.

Tanahashi was clearly always going to be a major star. In his twenties, he had a muscular build and a pretty boy look with dyed blond hair and just the slightest air of arrogance that could make hardcore male fans both hate and love him at the drop of a hat, and crucially, women and children fawn over him. As NJPW struggled badly at the box office, the audience was rapidly aging into a predominantly middle-aged male fanbase who had stuck with the company since the golden years. Tanahashi would help to change that dynamic, but it would take some time. Unlike Nakamura, he wasn't a BJJ enthusiast with MMA aspirations; he was a devotee of Fujinami, adopting his Dragon Suplex as a finish before adding a spectacular frog splash he dubbed the High Fly Flow.

A hard worker, but with a style that was out of fashion with company brass, he was instead given a new belt to work with; the U-30 Championship for competitors under the age of 30 regardless of weight class. While the title would be dropped by 2006, after only having two holders in history (Tanahashi and Nakamura, in fact) the title created some interesting matchups for those yearning for a return to traditional pro wrestling. It helped that it gave younger talent, including the promising Hiroki Goto and Toru Yano (who surprisingly given his later character, was billed as a serious mat wrestler building on his strong amateur background initially), something to do.

Tanahashi would mould his character through excursions, including to America where he worked with NWA offshoot TNA, and rise to stardom in the second half of the decade, while Nakamura would undergo more radical changes. Still, two out of the three musketeers looked to have a rise to fame that paralleled their forebears. Though the analogues would shift somewhat later on, Nakamura was the legit shooter, the Hashimoto of the group. Tanahashi was the athletic Muto, meanwhile. It was the potential leading heel, Shibata, that had a very different path.

In addition to the U-30 Championship, NJPW dabbled with bringing back the Young Lion Cup in the early 2000s, running the tournament four times between 2000 and 2005. The final winner would be Shibata's high school classmate Goto, but the 2000 cup was a strong class. A 21 year old Shibata was joined by Tanahashi, Shinya Makabe (Better known as Togi later on), Wataru Inoue, who would have a decent if unremarkable run in the company in years to come before retiring due to neck issues in 2014, eventual winner Kenzo Suzuki (a mediocre wrestler, Suzuki would have a run in WWE in the mid 2000s before working with AJPW and currently Muto's Wrestle-1), and former WAR talent Masakazu Fukuda.

Fukuda had worked with NJPW in 1999 before suffering a sudden brain hemorrhage. He had emergency surgery and recovered, passing all medical tests to return to the ring. April 14 2000 saw Fukuda wrestle his first match since the surgery. He exchanged forearm shots with Shibata, and some basic maneuvers, before Shibata hit an elbow drop near Fukuda's head. Fukuda didn't kick out of the ensuing pinfall attempt like he was supposed to. He never woke up, passing away of a second hemorrhage three days later.

Shibata's departure in the midst of a push to prominence made him unpopular with peers. *Photo: Yukio Hiraku/AFLO*

The incident was in no way Shibata's fault, but he would have to carry the memory with him going forward, and with little accountability taken by anyone within New Japan at large, company image fell further. Nonetheless, Shibata would progress through the Young Lion Cup to embody the hard-hitting character that NJPW wanted to fill, even if it meant potentially dangerous strikes in a medium that should have been more concerned for performer safety, especially as shoot experiments continued. Shibata would have opportunities at the IWGP Junior Heavyweight, and with Inoue, tag team titles. While he lost both, he seemed in line for a heavy push into the mid 2000s. Then, after becoming increasingly unhappy and frustrated at his position in the company, he abruptly left. October 2004 saw the first time that the New Three Musketeers teamed together, in a Korakuen Hall main event. Three months later, stating that he 'didn't want to be a salaryman wrestler', Shibata walked out on his contract, working with NOAH and forming a tag team with close friend 'KENTA' Kobayashi, before experimenting with MMA independently from NJPW.

If there were shining lights in the lower end of a NJPW card, it was all ruined by the bizarre approach to booking main event stars. Here there were repeated MMA matches that saw wrestlers get obliterated; there, worked bouts with fighters that had no aptitude for pulling their punches. There was no creative stability, and no consistency, a reflection of what was going on in the company behind the scenes. Frightened at being potentially booked into dangerous shoot fights, Keiji Muto, former IWGP Junior champion Kendo Kashin and Satoshi Kojima all left NJPW in January 2002 and headed to All Japan, with whom relations had once again turned hostile. Riki Choshu was blamed for the exodus, publicly slammed the company in an interview, and was fired.

Chono took over booking duties in NJPW, and for the most part was a voice of reason, whose traditional booing philosophies lead to Nagata and Takayama being given lengthy title runs, and Tenzan having his long years of service rewarded with the IWGP belt. Chono and Inoki frequently butted heads, though, with the majority shareholder insistent on forcing Chono to persist with the vale tudo style, MMA fighters, and poor ideas like the returning NWF belt.

More strange decisions, included throwing large sums of money toward Hulk Hogan to wrestle his last, extremely limited, Japanese match with Chono, which served as the backdrop to an angle involving Jeff Jarrett from TNA. The former WWF and WCW star assaulted Hogan at the after show press conference to set up a match that never happened. At least Hogan had a history in Japan; former WWF Intercontinental champion Chyna, who regardless of a lack of in-ring aptitude had arguably done much to challenge perceptions of female talent in the US, just wasn't a fit in NJPW. Despite Chono doing his best with her, the ensuing matches with the now renamed, and with a growing substance abuse problem, Chynna Doll were critical and commercial failures.

Inoki, meanwhile, showed signs of wanting out of the company he created. Seeking to spark speculation that could lead to a rise in value of the company he could sell out and cash in on, he told the Tokyo Sports newspaper that he had sold his majority stake in New Japan to K1 official Kazuyoshi Ishii. The newspaper ran the story on its front page on February 1 2002, forcing an incensed Chono to hastily stage a press conference to state that the story was categorically untrue, and that Inoki's move to sell could only happen with the consent of the company's entire board. Later in 2002, Inoki attempted to sell NJPW's tape library, this time to Vince McMahon; this had to be harshly blocked by TV Asahi who had to remind Inoki that the tape library was theirs, not his to sell.

An increasingly disinterested Inoki handed over a lot of duties to his son Simon, whose poor decisions didn't help ease NJPW's financial issues. He continued to push money behind the LA dojo that opened in 2002, which, while bringing stars like Bryan Danielson, Karl Anderson, Rocky Romero and Fergal Devitt through its doors, and being established in a bid to create new foreign stars for the company in the vein of Scott Norton, (a reliable hand for the company who was given a pair of IWGP Championship reigns), was a loss leader to put it mildly.

Scott Norton's long loyalty to New Japan was appreciated by the fans and company *Photo: Yukio Hiraku/AFLO*

Tenzan produced stirling work while carrying the IWGP championship, but had little hope of turning business around. *Photo: Yukio Hiraku/AFLO*

He would also be blamed for a debacle involving the loss of the IWGP championship from the company and the ill-advised saga of Brock Lesnar in the coming years. Often teasing that he himself would head to the LA Dojo to add mass and get in the ring, the self aggrandising Inoki Junior was not well liked within the company, and a poor figure at the head as finances dwindled.

Satoshi Kojima returned to NJPW in early 2005 as Triple Crown champion and ended Tenzan's second IWGP title reign to become a double champion in Ryogoku. It should have been a big money angle, and it was a dramatic match, with an ending more than 50 minutes in of Tenzan getting knocked out and the referee stopping the match. Regardless of both stars' talent, a May 5 2005 Tokyo Dome rematch between the two former partners was never going to fill the building, especially after a poor wrestling v MMA themed January 4 show.

Out of tradition, stubbornness or stupidity, the Dome was booked. To support the main, there was a legends tag match, Chono and Liger teaming opposite Fujinami shortly before he left the company and Mitsuharu Misawa on loan from NOAH. NOAH drew 50,000 plus to the Dome in July that year. The May NJPW show had a record low 21,000. Gates were appalling.

With finances circling the drain, Simon Inoki and crew prepared to close up shop and sell off assets to a selection of third party creditors. The King of Sports looked to have gone from the throne to the gutter.

Moving Merchandise

Merchandise is as important to a wrestling company in Japan as anywhere else, and NJPW's merchandising history tells its own tale of fluctuating fortunes for the company.

Japanese wrestling merchandise for the most part is similar to material from western promotions these days, and a walk into the numerous wrestling themed shops in Suidobashi near the Tokyo Dome and Korakuen Hall will reveal the expected array of T-shirts and action figures. NJPW's iconic lion mark logo was the centerpiece of merch from the 1970s on, and the white and red lion shirt would eventually be joined by wrestler specific apparel as talent and the company realised their potential as revenue streams.

Today's output is very much indicative of NJPW's desire to be in the mainstream of entertainment and sports media, even compared to the material sold at live events less than a decade ago. English slogans now make sense for the most part (in wrestling's strange world, where bold letters proclaiming a shirt wearer 'KING OF STRONG STYLE' or exclaiming 'Loose Explosion!' isn't hideously embarrassing, anyway) and are inoffensive. Yujiro Takahashi's T shirt that proclaimed 'WE RUN SHIT', or even more bluntly in the mid 2000's, a Jado and Gedo shirt that simply read 'FUCK YOU- WE'RE JADO AND GEDO' are a thing of the past.

NJPW's recovering fortunes have also lead to cross-branding opportunities with mainstream characters. While a recent cross over that saw shirts featuring stylized wrestlers reimagined as characters from wrestling manga/ anime *Kinnikuman* was unsurprising, cross overs with Sanrio and Disney that saw the lion mark shirts tweaked to feature Mickey Mouse and Hello Kitty were more remarkable sights, and crucially big sellers to women and children while Shinsuke Nakamura and the Bullet Club would bring in cash from young adult males.

Wrestling albums were an international merchandising curio in the '70s, and stars from both sides of the Pacific would try their hands at crooning into a microphone with often humorous results. While Terry Funk and Bruiser Brody both had their own records while touring with All Japan, NJPW's stars were rather more restrained, Antonio Inoki releasing a spoken word album that couldn't touch Funk reminiscing about the girls in Roppongi or his amazing disco theme. Hulk Hogan's *Ichiban*, released during his 1983 NJPW tour is much more like it, the title track containing such lyrics as 'Hulk Hogan is his name, action action is his game'.

More interesting, and unique to Japan, was NJPW's early home video output. While western companies took a while to realise the sales potential of VHS tapes of events, NJPW were steadily trickling out match highlight tapes early in the '80s, albeit at ludicrously high prices of up to 10,000 Yen (roughly 100 USD, pre-inflation) per event. NJPW were also on the cutting edge of laser disc technology, releasing best of compilations on the failed format in glorious collector boxes, as well as a complete collection of the *Azteckaiser* series.

While DVD and BluRay copies of event footage has been a steady presence in recent years (albeit overpriced in a country where physical optical media remains popular and expensive), many features focussed on a particular wrestler or group take more of a personality piece approach. A semi-regular NJPW DVD magazine series ran through the mid 2000s and simply followed wrestlers on their days off away from the ring, going to restaurants or go-kart tracks. Toru Yano, meanwhile, has a series of DVDs that follow him and Chaos teammates that focus on personalities away from the ring, with a series of skits at hot springs or in high school cosplay, only barely touching on philosophies within it. There's a sense then, that fans of NJPW's in-ring product already are attending live events and watching TV; people buying extra products are looking for something more.

Videogames have been a big source of licensing income for wrestling companies in recent years, but NJPW came to the medium relatively late, allowing Fujicom to develop NJPW *Challenge in Tokyo Dome* well into the 1990s, and a pair of further titles named after the *Battlefield* January 4th show on PC Engine and Super Famicom. The games certainly drew visual attention to the stars with big detailed sprites as compared to more stylized cartoonish visuals in licensed All Japan efforts, but they weren't much to play.

From 1995 to 2000, game production fell to Osaka based developer Yuke's and published by toy manufacturers Tomy Takara. The partnership produced four games under the *Tokon Retsuden* (Road of Fighting Spirit) name on Playstation, N64 and Dreamcast formats. At the same time AKI Corporation included a small selection of stars like Inoki, Liger and Tiger Mask in the first two installments of their classic *Virtual Pro Wrestling* series thanks to NJPW's working relationship at the time with WCW, from whom those games were licensed. *Retsuden* produced decent, if slightly stodgy efforts, though AJPW had a better time critically and financially with their game licensing, reaping rewards from further collaboration with AKI and publisher Asmik Ace for *Virtual Pro Wrestling* 2, and a Sega still influential in the industry with a trio of strong arcade based outings.

In the early 2000s, individual wrestling game licenses were of less value as live gates began to dwindle, leading to games with diverse cross promotional rosters. Square Enix produced a trio of *All Star Wrestling* titles that featured NJPW, AJPW and NOAH, promotions banding together in a manner that wouldn't likely happen in other markets. Meanwhile Spike produced the *King of Colosseum* games which also included Zero One and independent stars. The second of these allowed you to book the promotion of your choice; it wasn't likely that you'd do a worse job than the various combinations of Inoki, Choshu and Chono at the time.

There were some NJPW specific offerings from this time period, but, apart from the limited release of *Tokon Retsuden Advance* by Tomy, they were non-traditional efforts developed by Pacific Century Cyberworks, a massive Chinese telecommunications company that had a game development arm. The first, *Tokon Inoki Michi Puzzle De Da!* On Playstation 2, bizarrely saw caricatures of Inoki and 2001 NJPW talent such as Masahiro Chono and Hiroshi Tenzan square off in a contest to see who could arrange falling gems in like coloured groups. Bombs would clear away groups and unleash signature maneuvers on opponents in a decent game, albeit one copied wholesale from Capcom's *Super Puzzle Fighter*. There was also *Tokon Heat* on GBA, which took a more role-playing approach with players strategically choosing from a list of moves during a match. That game was supposed to make a cross media star out of the central Heat character, but this never really took off as we discovered earlier.

The NJPW gaming license became the sole property of Yuke's in 2005, as the developer found themselves owning a majority share of the company. They produced a spiritual successor to the *Tokon Retsuden* series with a lot of that game's original development team, and called it *Wrestle Kingdom*, releasing in late 2005 alongside the Japanese launch of Microsoft's XBox 360. A serviceable title with a campaign centered around taking a rookie character from Young Lion to IWGP champion, the game struggled at retail, with its host platform being unpopular in Japan, though a later PS2 port did better.

To promote the sequel, which would improve on in-ring mechanics and have a broader roster of current and legendary figures, Yuke's rebranded NJPW's January 4th Tokyo Dome show as Wrestle Kingdom, a name that has stuck to this day. Still, with combined sales of both games barely scraping over 20,000 copies, retail performance painted a grim picture of the relevance of the NJPW brand in the mid 2000s. Even as fortunes slowly began to recover prior to Yuke's selling their NJPW share to Bushiroad in 2012, development cost of videogames outstripped any reward they might receive.

Bushiroad is predominantly a company that makes trading card games, and assorted media like kid's cartoon shows around them. *Vanguard* and *Buddyfight* are popular collectible card games amongst pre-teens, and the company's accrual of NJPW allowed them to produce a CCG that would appeal to an older audience. King of Pro Wrestling debuted in the autumn of 2012, along with a Wrestle Kingdom like event in Sumo Hall named after it, and is a consistent if unremarkable seller.

Meanwhile, after an eight year hiatus, NJPW returned to a virtual wrestling ring in summer 2015 with a title dubbed *Pro Wrestling Yaroze* (let's play pro-wrestling), this time taking a free to play approach with small real money transactions taking place in game, a model that reaps more rewards from modest development costs. Apparel from Tshirts to hoodies and towels have recently been made available in markets outside of Japan, making for some strong selling items. We've even had a return of New Japan wrestlers to the recording studio as Toru Yano produced and sang on a Chaos CD that included a traditional *enka* styled tune with lyrics wondering how Gedo can see straight with his bandana on. What's old is new again.

10

Roadblocks to Redemption

Yuke's Company Ltd. was established in 1993, a video game developer that quickly made a reputation as a sturdy, reliable producer of work made to order for licensors of TV shows and other properties. Among their early output were games based on the *Uchannachan no Hono no Challenger* prime time game show, and indeed NJPW, with the *Tokon Retsuden* series of games.

Their work on the latter would see them catch the eye of American toy company turned game publisher THQ, who put Yuke's to work on a WCW game before licenses changed hands, and the WCW title turned into *WWF Smackdown!* in 1999. The WWF/WWE license became Yuke's bread and butter in the coming years, and saw the company grow, develop and become able to create their own properties, which would largely be poorly received.

Influxes of cash saw rapid expansion of the company, which saw a spin-off Yuke's Media Creations publishing arm for games and other media. They would publish WWE's DVD output in Japan through the mid 2000s, and it was thus, three years after Inoki attempted to sell NJPW's tape library to WWE, that Vince McMahon indirectly bankrolled the purchase of New Japan Pro Wrestling.

The exact price that 54% of NJPW was bought for on November 30, 2005 was never made public, though media dubbed it a firesale with creditors looming. Simon Inoki, for his part, called the purchase 'a blessing' in subsequent interviews, likely aware that he was well out of his depth as captain of a sinking ship.

Under Yuke's corporate direction, the younger Inoki was still acting president, but had to comply with the new owners' edict; redouble on wrestling, eliminate vale tudo, and dramatically reduce spending. It would lead to a lean few years, and a departure of talent and executives upset at the direction of the company. The feeling was that a non-wrestling organization with majority ownership was arguably attempting to fatten NJPW up for sale, and the struggling and unpopular president still being in charge didn't help. Hiro Saito, along with former *Ishingun* member from way back in the '80s Tatsutoshi Goto, along with Hidekazu Tanaka, (who was a high ranking office staff member, and known to the fans as a long serving ring announcer for the company), all opted not to renew contracts and would leave in early 2006.

If the pay roll was shrinking somewhat with the turnover, there was a big, and very expensive addition made to it prior to Yuke's involvement that would cause some headaches heading into 2006. Brock Lesnar had left WWE in the spring of 2004, burned out on that promotion's travel schedule, and with the hopes of forging a career in American football. Unable to find a spot in a prominent team, Lesnar would turn down the option of playing in the NFL's European league, instead opting to return to wrestling, and then forge a path in MMA. The young Inoki swooped, despite Lesnar's high price tag; a recognisable American name with a legitimate amateur wrestling background, he could be a big hand in both pro wrestling and vale tudo matches, and a giant with, in theory, a highly marketable look.

Lesnar was hot shotted directly into the main event of another show inexplicably booked at the Tokyo Dome on October 8 2005. In a first for the company, Lesnar joined Masahiro Chono in challenging for the IWGP title in a three way match against now two time champion Kazuyuki Fujita. In a show that drew a dismal 16,000 fans, Lesnar won the title, dropping Chono with what western fans knew as his F5 finisher, renamed Verdict in Japan due to WWE owning the 'F5' rights, and as a reference to an ongoing legal dispute between Lesnar and WWE who claimed the new IWGP champion was infringing on a no-compete clause in his old contract.

That no-compete clause would lead to concerns over the winter that an injunction may leave NJPW without a champion. Nevertheless, he was still booked in defences up to the spring of 2006, costing the company money they didn't have and not moving the needle when it came to drawing punters. Part of the issue was that Lesnar showed a clear lack of motivation in-ring, arguably having lost his passion for the business after his departure from WWE. He would put in subpar, slow paced performances that rarely lasted over ten minutes, and this in the main event of shows, whether against skilled opponents like Shinsuke Nakamura, or limited ones (former sumo yokozuna Chad 'Akebono' Rowan, who was trying to segue out of sumo into a pro career, earning Japanese headlines for a publicity stunt sumo match with Big Show at WWE's Wrestlemania 21, and subsequently adopted by Japanese promotions who didn't get the message of WWE opting for a sumo bout to disguise Akebono's significant athletic shortcomings and lack of mobility).

Lesnar was a poor choice of champion from a business standpoint, and in terms of merchandise. Yuke's realised this: capitalising on the purchase of the company, they released a new videogame on the Playstation 2 and newly launched XBox 360 called *Wrestle Kingdom* with Lesnar front and centre on the cover, and while the business being in a poor state was mostly to blame, the title sold terribly. Yuke's imposed a number of austerity measures in 2006; firstly, the Tokyo Dome would be run once a year, and only once a year on January 4 (and would carry the same name as their poorly selling game franchise). Meanwhile, Lesnar as champion couldn't last, with the company instead set to be booked around a homegrown ace: Hiroshi Tanahashi. On 19 March 2006, after Lesnar defeated Akebono in a plodding bout with a DDT to a flat reaction, Tanahashi challenged the future UFC champion. A match was put in place for later in the summer, but never happened.

Complications over Lesnar's visa were blamed by NJPW for his no-show, and instead a tournament was held for the now vacant IWGP championship, which Tanahashi won. Embarrassingly though, Lesnar had the physical belt, and refused to relinquish it, claiming that the company owed him pay. It was an embarrassment that wouldn't be resolved for another year, and most of the blame was put on Inoki's shoulders.

Yet Simon Inoki remained a bullish president, surviving votes of confidence from shareholders. Inoki would soon reinstall Riki Choshu to book the promotion despite his public outburst after being fired in 2002. If anything, Choshu gained more freedoms within the company. He would even be allowed to start his own spinoff promotion featuring NJPW and independent stars, under the Wrestleland Lock-up! name, which seemed oddly similar to the Zero concept Hashimoto had pitched to him before being let go years prior.

To the frustration of many, Inoki was once again re-elected president at the company shareholder meeting in 2006. Fujinami issued an ultimatum to other officials; him or the Inoki/Choshu combination. Fujinami resigned, and with Hiro Saito, Tatsutoshi Goto and Hidekazu Tanaka started his own independent promotion Muga, which would become Dradition and run Tokyo shows every few months.

Finally, and to the relief of many, Inoki announced he would step down as president in April 2007, turning over company reigns to long-term front office employee Naoki Sugabayashi. Oddly enough, the same day Simon Inoki announced his decision to leave, his father announced he was getting back into the pro wrestling game with the Inoki Genome Federation. The promotion would see Inoki's dreams of having an MMA/pro wrestling hybrid company come to pass without any interfering financial officers or miserable punters. IGF would ultimately run occasional shows to modest crowds, but opened with much hype, and the announcement of one Brock Lesnar defending one IWGP title in its debut main event.

The Inokis also signed up Lesnar's former WWE running buddy and Olympic gold medallist Kurt Angle to work with Lesnar. Finally working against someone he had decent chemistry with, Lesnar turned in the best performance of his Japanese career before dropping the 'real' IWGP title to Angle. By this point, Kurt was wrestling for TNA in the States, who still had a working relationship with New Japan. Angle's appearance in this and subsequent shows meant that Inoki could have a big marquee main event, while NJPW could finally have ultimate control of both IWGP titles, staging a unification match on February 17 2008 with Shinsuke Nakamura.

While Ryogoku was nowhere near packed, the bout showed a refreshed and rejuvenated feel to NJPW at large, for better or worse no longer under any Inoki influence for the first time in the company's 35 year history. Nakamura submitted Angle with a cross arm breaker to become the undisputed IWGP champion.

The former 'Supernova' was in the midst of a change in character that over the coming years saw Nakamura transform from straight-laced jiu jitsu practitioner to the charismatic swagger of the King of Strong Style. Much like Chono and Muto in the 1990s, Nakamura and Tanahashi moved from tag partners, beating Kensuke Sasaki and Minoru Suzuki in December 2004, to bitter rivals, each bringing out the best in one another. The 'New Three Musketeers' dynamic had shifted; while Tanahashi had become a traditional ring general in the Chono mould, Nakamura was a magnetic, electrifying Muto-like personality.

After losing to Brock Lesnar in 2006, Nakamura had undergone an excursion to Mexico and South America, the traditional Young Lion rite of passage that had been denied him due to being pushed hard and fast into main events in his early 20s (the push happened so suddenly for Nakamura that many within the company feared a locker room revolt among other young talents; when given long shorts as ring gear instead of traditional Young Lion garb, he was told to hide his outfit until the last possible second). Returning that autumn, he was put into a prominent role in Chono's Black stable, a follow-up on the nWo and Team 2000 gimmicks that played on creative tugs of war between Choshu and Chono; the idea being that Black would seize control of NJPW, installing Chono as its president and Nakamura as its top star.

Chono, for his part, was winding down in his career after one final G1 Climax victory in 2005, and a final run with the IWGP tag titles with Tenzan. Under the Black banner, Nakamura wrestled All Japan's Toshiaki Kawada at the first Wrestle Kingdom show in 2007 in a hard hitting bout that did a lot even in defeat to solidify him as a top star.

A dislocated shoulder in that summer's G1 Climax against Yuji Nagata saw Nagata advance to the finals of the tournament by stoppage. Tanahashi, bleeding from the elbow and mouth would win that year, while Nakamura was sidelined for three months. On his return, though, he was pushed equally as hard, taking control of Black from a departing Chono and renaming the faction RISE.

The dress code implicit in his prior faction's title gone, Nakamura for the most part dropped the MMA like gear he had been wearing, instead opting for long red tights. He started growing his hair out, and was becoming more distinct from the rest of the roster, adding in a few more arrogant mannerisms and a spring in his step gleaned from a lifelong fandom of Freddy Mercury and Michael Jackson.

Tanahashi meanwhile was the prototypical ace, standing alone without the need of a stable of wrestlers as his backup, and a figure who had earned main event credibility with fans after his initial IWGP championship reign started inauspiciously as a result of Lesnar's departure. Helping to establish Tanahashi was Yuji Nagata, who had ridden out the damage his MMA career had done to become one of the most respected veterans to NJPW talent and fans, who could work with, and make a star of, almost anyone.

The two would work with one another through much of 2007, Tanahashi's first title reign ended by Nagata in April, and the younger talent victorious in the G1 final in August before an October rubber match saw Tanahashi win the IWGP championship for a second time. It was a series brilliantly strung together as a trilogy of main events, and showed a talent Tanahashi in particular would display in his time on top in NJPW of working with the same opponent several times and tell an evolving story across a series. By the time of the third bout that October in Sumo Hall, Tanahashi's pretty boy poses to the crowd in between working over Nagata's knee were getting cheers of grudging respect from the audience rather than boos of anger at his cockiness.

Tanahashi and Nakamura main evented the Tokyo Dome Wrestle Kingdom 2 in 2008, wrestling for the IWGP Heavyweight championship for the first time then, and in the midst of a rivalry that was still in its early years. To watch matches between the two over the course of a decade is to see the two characters and human beings evolve in scrapbook fashion, and WK2's main event was a story of two stars just approaching their peak years.

Already knowing each other well as partners and opponents, it was a match full of counters, and the story of Nakamura's will to win shone through. He'd grab Tanahashi's ankle in a desperate bid to stop him hitting a decisive High Fly Flow and instead hit a sit out Michinoku Driver variant he called the Landslide from the top rope and once more in the middle of the ring to win. It was a dramatic match that would only be improved by more maturity in the main event scene from both men. Tanahashi would soon shed the arrogant young posturing and become a self-appointed locker room leader, while Nakamura gained even more of an explosive aggressiveness and unique sense of character as leader of yet another stable spun off from RISE, dubbed Chaos.

The idea of a roster divided into factions was one NJPW had dabbled with since *Ishingun* in the 80's, and became more entranced by during the mid 90's nWo heyday. In the wake of NJPW returning to its pro wrestling roots, stables of wrestlers sprung up all over the card, which had its positives and drawbacks.

For one, it created a complex entangled spider web of alliances and rivalries closer to the episodic 'sports entertainment' drama of western wrestling companies. As talent joined and left factions, it made for a product harder for new fans to just jump into and watch. A counter argument was that it still felt like a sports style product, but with individual wrestlers part of a team, or the fight camps of MMA; talent that teamed together in the case of a big dispute, but that weren't necessarily focused on taking down the established wrestling system like the nWo or Black were presented as doing. A big positive of booking stables was that emphasis could be placed on younger talent otherwise lost in the mix, as they could be called on in eight or ten man tag team main events on spot shows and given a chance to show what they were capable of.

As previously mentioned, CTU was a fine platform to draw attention to Prince Devitt, and a young Hiroki Goto, who would go on to be the 2008 G1 winner. A hard hitter in the Sasaki mould, Goto had an arsenal of moves targeting the neck, and an occasional ill-advised tendency to openly headbutt opponents with no protective hand to the temple, the hollow thud of skulls echoing sickeningly around arenas. To many a critic, Goto was and would continue to be thereabouts, but never there, challenging and being defeated by IWGP champions consistently over the coming years and rarely receiving faith that he could be someone more than a supporting player. Yet Goto is still a respected hand, exceptional with the right opponent, and with a flair for intricate work as well as rough housing, often performing complicated rope running with opponents in a bid to misdirect the audience.

CTU dissolved on August 8 2007, an occasion that saw members all don masks to become CTU Rangers, a play on popular *Power Rangers* style kids TV shows. Its members, cannily, weren't sent out to fend for themselves as singles when not necessarily ready, and many former CTU talent would join Black members in Nakamura's RISE.

Real International Super Elite might have been a slightly tortuous English acronym, but it served as a strong base for development. Goto was able to ply his trade further before striking out alone. Devitt too, who having come through the LA and then Tokyo New Japan dojo was embraced by the fans as their own despite coming from abroad, in the same way Chris Benoit had earned the Japanese audience's respect in the early '90s.

Joining them in RISE was a range of Japanese and international talent, junior and heavyweight. Minoru Tanaka was there, recovering from a run as the underwhelming Heat, along with Milano Collection

A.T., a promising junior who had started with Dragon Gate precursor Toryumon and won the 2007 Best of the Super Junior tournament. Milano's future with NJPW seemed bright before his career abruptly ended after vision issues following a kick to the head from Jado in a 2010 match, but he would remain involved in the company in the office and as an announcer for Samurai TV. Giant Bernard was already a veteran on entry to the group; the huge Matt Bloom had already enjoyed a lengthy run as the somewhat poorly named Prince Albert (later, mercifully, just 'Albert' and then A Train) in WWE, before heading to All and then New Japan, and forming a tag team with another former WWE star, Travis 'Tyson' Tomko.

While Bernard and Tomko made for an imposing team in RISE, it was with Bloom's second partner that he garnered more success. Karl Anderson came to NJPW having trained in the LA Dojo, and made a respectable name for himself on the US independent circuit. With Tomko leaving due to budget cuts, Anderson was a cheaper proposition, and had excellent chemistry with Bernard. With the tag team scene in NJPW pushed to the background as the company desperately tried to create new singles stars, Bad Intentions would be a staple between 2008 and 2012, including an 18 month reign with the IWGP Tag championships starting in the summer of 2010.

Yet it wasn't in RISE that Bernard and Anderson encountered one another, but yet another stable, Togi Makabe's Great Bash Heel. GBH had been formed in 2006 by Tenzan in the wake of his breaking up with Chono as a tag partner, with the aim to have a faction of brawling hard hitters. Togi Makabe, no longer the straight-laced Shinya, had reinvented himself as the 'Unchained Gorilla', a hardcore brawling tribute to his icon Bruiser Brody. Like Brody, he stormed to the ring with chains around his neck to a cover of Led Zeppelin's Immigrant Song, and utilised a 'King Kong' knee drop to defeat opponents.

Settled into his new character, Makabe would receive a heavy push, becoming leader of GBH as Tenzan left to briefly tour All Japan, and having a fantastic match with Nakamura en route to winning the 2009 G1 Climax.

Makabe was given a heroic story through the final night of the tournament in Ryogoku, his semi final match with Takashi Sugiura, who was on loan from NOAH, being a bloody affair that saw him contest the finals with a bandaged head. Nakamura would rip the bandage from Makabe's wound, making a sympathetic figure out of the supposed heel. Nakamura laid in strikes to Makabe's head, who repeatedly fired up before hitting a pair of King Kong knees for the win. It was a dramatic bout that turned Makabe into a respected fan favourite, and foreshadowed the later destruction of GBH and the foundation of Chaos.

Makabe would also have a run as tag team champion with surprising partner Toru Yano. Yano's amateur background wasn't really translating itself as sellable to the audience and he would undergo a transformation in 2005 into a brawling based character who would take any shortcut necessary. Yano's paunchy physique that could only be earned by being a heavyweight drinker as well as a heavyweight wrestler (on November 12, 2012, Yano opened a sports bar called Ebrietas in Suidobashi, a stone's throw from Korakuen Hall and the Tokyo Dome) eventually made him an adorable comedy figure to the fans. for the time being, the Most Violent Players tag team were a fine brutal pairing in the Hansen/Brody vein.

GBH would also play host to the veteran tag team of Jado and Gedo. As NJPW parted ways with both Choshu, as funding for his Lockup side project was halted, and Chono, who was gradually becoming a regular as a figure on panel comedy shows and kids' TV, the pair gradually found themselves assuming more responsibilities, before ascending to roles as bookers within the organisation. Under their regime, sweeping changes to the NJPW roster eliminated any vestiges of the vale tudo era. While MMA philosophies when it came to presentation and promotion were kept, presenting homogenous wrestlers with kick pads, fight gear and no underlying character was out. Instead every NJPW wrestler gained their own unique personality, making them more marketable and the product more appealing.

The brusque 'unchained gorilla' was a perfect character for the brawling Makabe *Photo: Yukio Hiraku/AFLO*

Yano had already gone from serious wrestler to bleached blonde hardcore brawler. GBH stablemate Takashi Iizuka was no longer the straight-laced star who beat Choshu on the night of his retirement but never seemed to benefit. Instead he'd grow out his beard, shave his head and gain an entrance through the crowd, scattering furniture and fans as he went. The bland Mitsuhide Hirasawa first became the bizarre Hideo Saito, who often teamed with Iizuka and had a similar wild man gimmick, though with his grown out beard and filthy clothes, seemed more like a homeless individual than a pro wrestler. He would then transform into

Captain New Japan, a child friendly heroic mascot for the company, who would lose every match in comic fashion.

With everybody encouraged to find their own character, or have one assigned to them, each wrestler brought something fresh to the show, as well as the stables they were in, meaning that the nWo syndrome of placing a generic T-shirt on a star in a bid to attach them to a bandwagon was dropped in favour of everyone playing a unique role. GBH expanded to bring in a pair of figures who had drawn NJPW's attention after working outside of the company. Tomoaki Honma had forged a career in Big Japan Pro Wrestling, working numerous deathmatch bouts, that left him scarred and with crushed vocal chords making his speech almost inaudible. Teaming with Makabe, he was able to soften his weapon heavy approach and eventually become a phenomenally popular underdog figure. Tomohiro Ishii, meanwhile, had worked for various companies in the late '90s and early 2000s, including WAR, Toryumon and Zero One, and in GBH slowly started to develop respect as someone willing to work through all manner of injuries, but that would hit terrifyingly hard.

Not every stable created was successful, or even memorable. As Tenzan returned from All Japan to find Makabe in full control of GBH, he would join a Legends faction that also included Satoshi Kojima, meaning they were able to reform their tag team. Beyond that, this was a holding cell for Chono as he left in-ring competition, and Liger, who by this point was a locker room leader working with young talent in opening matches, his heyday long behind.

Similarly Yuji Nagata's *Seigigun* (lit. 'Justice army') did little for Wataru Inoue, the young Mitsuhide Hirasawa before ascending to the rank of Captain, or a Super Strong Machine appearing purely for nostalgia purposes. It would start a tough few years for Nagata from 2009 on, who coming off of his IWGP reigns that did so much for Tanahashi, and similarly great matches with Kurt Angle and Zero One's Masato Tanaka, was in the wilderness, being phased out due to his age but still feeling he had more to contribute.

Nagata's role in Zero One cross promotion lead to some excellent work with Masato Tanaka. *Photo: Yukio Hiraku/AFLO*

In working with both Angle and Tanaka, as well as subsequent years of being on loan to NOAH, Nagata was an ambassador of sorts for NJPW. More out of attrition and the more stable Yuke's corporate backing than out of phenomenal business (new, positive creative direction aside, business was by no means good, weekly TV still resolutely in a brief late night slot, and Wrestle Kingdom cards drawing around 20,000 fans to the Dome in the latter half of the decade), NJPW found itself at the top of a domestically flagging industry and faltering economy.

While starting to develop its own stars, the company was able to bring in already established names from foreign companies by trading on prior reputation, relationships with TNA providing Angle and Team 3D, and a working relationship with CMLL in Mexico bringing a host of talent to Japan for one month a year under the Fantasticamania banner. As a result, Japanese audiences were introduced to Mistico prior to a disastrous run as Sin Cara in WWE, and NJPW were later able to make extended use of talent like La Sombra and Mascara Dorada. The company also maintained territories for talent to have learning excursions in this way; Taichi Ishikari and Prince Devitt and Nakamura all heading to CMLL, while TNA saw brief appearances by Tanahashi and a longer run for Kazuchika Okada.

The young Tokyo resident was initially trained by Ultimo Dragon in Toryumon before starting again in an NJPW dojo class that also included Tetsuya Naito and Yujiro Takahashi, who themselves would form an '80s throwback styled tag team called No Limit before going their separate ways. Okada was very much given the Young Lion losing routine for most of 2009, before slowly starting to gain traction, forming a short lived tag team with HIroki Goto, before receiving a mini push in early 2010. He'd even be given a short match with Tanahashi that January, as a prelude to leaving to work in TNA. Okada might have started to emerge from the shadow of being another black underwear clad body in NJPW, but TNA had little creative direction for him whatsoever, pairing him with veteran Samoa Joe in an ill advised tandem that was based around a forgettable *Green Lantern* movie. He would come back reinvigorated to say the least.

With companies closer to home meanwhile, NJPW were embattled industry leaders. In the 1990s, collaborations with other companies were seen as a matter of the rising tide assisting all ships; now it was a case of everybody banding together in a desperate bid to hold heads above water. A group of companies once hostile to one another were united, often under tragic circumstances. Zero One, a modest success at first with Hashimoto and talented all rounder Masato Tanaka as Japanese talents and Steve Corino and the aforementioned Samoa Joe amongst its highly rated foreign roster was beset by its founder's sudden death on July 11 2005.

The company was already spiralling into debt, and Hashimoto had planned to help alleviate financial woes by working again with his alma mater NJPW on his return from a shoulder injury. The legendary former

IWGP champion was beset by blood pressure issues in addition to his injury however, and years of a very high impact style not typically compatible with his overweight form compounded things. Hashimoto had complained about chest pains for a few weeks and had suffered from sleep apnea, before abruptly collapsing on July 11 from a brain hemorrhage. He was just 40 years old.

In the wake of his death, Zero One was in further turmoil, without its founder, or finances. Hustle, a comedic sister wrestling promotion to the PRIDE MMA organisation that Hashimoto also had a large hand in was similarly crippled before funding scandals brought its parent company Dream Stage Entertainment down.

NOAH, another promotion with a strong start, was similarly beleaguered. After a strong opening built around the still growing legends of founder Mitsuharu Misawa and Kenta Kobashi, the promotion was starting to falter. TV ratings with NTV stalled, and as Misawa and Kobashi both aged, Kobashi taking time away for cancer treatment and not competing at the same level afterward, NOAH struggled to find a top drawing act. Kenta Kobayashi, billed as KENTA to avoid confusion with the main eventer and his mentor, Takeshi Morishima, Naomichi Marufuji, and more wrestlers like Jun Akiyama and Go Shiozaki who were part of the All Japan exodus were all excellent talents, but had little mainstream cache. The economic recession didn't help either, and NOAH's financial muscle was atrophying (and, as it turned out, with some shady mob backing). Then, on June 13 2009, five days before his 47th birthday, Misawa died in the ring after an Akitoshi Saito back suplex.

While the official cause of death was not made public, the general consensus was that it was the result of a severe injury to the spinal cord; in effect an internal decapitation. There was nothing wrong with Saito's performance of the move, though it was a dangerous maneuver to take, and Misawa, now years from his prime, had spent decades being dropped onto his head with dangerous moves.

Just as wrestling was under a critical eye in the west, as the murder/suicide case of Chris Benoit put into sharp focus issues with an industry that struggled to protect wrestlers from concussions and substance abuse, discussions took place about safety in Japan in the wake of Misawa's passing. The committee of education and science, appropriately enough headed at the time by Hiroshi Hase, summoned representatives of all major promotions, including Keiji Muto (who was by now president of an AJPW that faded fast from the public eye after Baba's passing), Naoki Sugabayashi for NJPW and Ryu Nakata, who took over NOAH's operations after Misawa's death.

Muto was in favour of a unified regulating body for all of pro wrestling. There was general talk of reducing the volume of moves targeting the head, having less blood involved in matches with HIV a concern. Referees would be officially licensed; doctors would be present at ringside. While this wasn't a government mandated issue that would affect every company, both large and small, discussions were necessary, and impacted the style of wrestling across the board in the country to change it into something safer, though not consistently so. Use of unprotected weapon shots to opponent's heads was effectively banned outside of violent promotions like BJW, but unprotected headbutts favoured by Goto and Ishii were allowed to happen unhindered. Doctors assessed wrestlers at ringside in NJPW, but often leniently, allowing Kota Ibushi to finish a June 2014 match with Kushida while clearly concussed, albeit giving him a lengthy time away to recover afterward.

Be it in dealing with talent safety, working under financial duress, or attracting the attention of the mainstream once more to what was once a weekly television and live institution, NJPW, and Japanese pro wrestling at large had a lot of obstacles to mount. Yet the next few years would see strong attempts to do so, and a brightening of the medium's future.

The New IWGP: What Next For NJPW Internationally?

We've seen how important foreign influences have been on Japanese pro wrestling, its talent and fans. Yet in a sense, for decades this was a one way street, or at least the return lane was a narrow one. Young Japanese talent would often head westward, but usually as part of a learning process, only rarely (in Chono and Liger's cases for WCW perhaps, or during the nWo Japan era) when already at the top of their games. Japanese shows themselves meanwhile had an aura of mystique to them perpetuated by a lack of access. Traded tapes - knowing someone who knew someone who had imported a VHS recorded from Japanese TV and was willing to make a copy - would be the only way to watch shows at all, presented in a foreign language and with a very different style of production than western fans were used to.

New Japan would have a limited presence in the 1990s in parts of mainland Europe. NOAH had a short-lived English language home at the Fight Network in Canada and the associated British Wrestling Channel. Still, Japanese pro wrestling and NJPW to foreign audiences was a niche within a niche, respected, but rarely followed, even into the current decade.

Yet in 2015, AXS TV's English localized version of TV Asahi's *World Pro Wrestling Returns*, which placed subtitled promos and commentary by Josh Barnett and Mauro Ranallo over the top of roughly year old NJPW matches (even the Japanese version of the show was six months behind current events, a delay New Japan were eager to close for 2016), became a hit for the network. It would, the host network claimed, frequently draw a 200,000 strong viewership (huge, given the channel's reach), often outdrawing domestically produced TV wrestling in the form of Ring of Honor or Lucha Underground in the US. Wrestle Kingdom 9, the company's first foray into traditional pay per view in international markets (not counting the closed circuit Inoki/Ali affair) was a modest success, with more than 12,000 purchasing the show.

NJPW talent, meanwhile, were immensely popular draws when added to international cards. This created a unique situation in summer 2015 where WWE booked Jushin Liger on a New York NXT card that just so happened to be running head-to-head with a Ring of Honor show (featuring Nakamura and Okada) in the same area - Japanese talent were in a position to act as heavy bargaining chips in an (anti) competitive battle for market share. What drove NJPW's burst in popularity in the West?

The book you're reading now was crowd funded via Indiegogo, creating a unique opportunity to directly poll wrestling fans, most of them in NJPW's biggest foreign markets of North America and Europe, on what attracted them to the New Japan product. The data within this chapter was provided by 206 respondents. While people who would purchase a book about NJPW history 'on spec' before release would skew to a hardcore wrestling audience, this is largely the demographic New Japan is targeting in the west at current, and fairly representative of their foreign audience.

93.37% of respondents follow New Japan on a regular basis, from 88.55% following WWE, 67.47% Ring of Honor, and 50.6% Mexico's AAA offshoot Lucha Underground. The portion of the audience that watches New Japan exclusively is incredibly small or non-existent, then, and speaks to a discerning audience for the promotion. What's worth mentioning is that other Japanese promotions fared poorly with respondents, with the most popular being NOAH at just 18.07%, and DDT and Dragon Gate trailing behind. There's a lot to be said about the relative quality of Japanese promotions in 2015, but it seems one key determining factor in NJPW's foreign appeal is simply accessibility.

While television would be the prime route for a promotion to enter people's homes in the past, there has been a shift of late. 43.5% of those polled prefer to use official streaming solutions to follow a wrestling product, with 27% heading to the TV first. That means that the WWE Network and NJPW World hold tremendous sway with the dedicated fan.

Other Japanese promotions do have streaming services. All Japan launched a service in mid 2015, and dedicated combat sports network Samurai TV started streaming that same summer. These services have their own drawbacks, with AJPW unable to secure classic archived footage, and Samurai being unavailable outside of Japan without a proxy network. Even if they were more appealing and accessible to a wider audience, though, these services would still likely struggle.

In the wake of WWE launching their network, and steadily building an audience of 1.3 million subscribers at time of writing, live streaming and Video On Demand (VOD) services from various wrestling companies sprang up in their droves. While a low price has been a selling point for most archival or live streaming services, it's arguable that consumer time, not money, is the biggest limiting factor for companies hoping to draw money on streaming subscriptions. 56.42% of survey respondents fell in the 25-35 demographic, with 29.61%, barely over half that number, between 18-25. Those over 35 numbered significantly fewer, which is typical (people between the ages of 18-34 are typically those with the biggest spending power online), but the slightly older skew towards an audience in their late 20s and early 30s suggests an audience with young families and other demands on their time. To that crowd, regularly subscribing, even at a low price, for hours of content they simply don't have time to watch, is a poor value proposition.

NJPW World's announcement in December 2014 might have seemed for all the world like bandwagon hopping. From Takaaki Kidani directly referencing the Network in his announcement of the service, to the 999 Yen monthly price point, it was aping WWE's approach to a tee. To the 72.56% of those polled that were World subscribers, the approach still worked, NJPW entering into the streaming market early enough, and with a strong enough package to convince those viewers to add another subscription to their regular diet of WWE Network, or to put their entire streaming budget behind New Japan. Still, the proportion of foreign subscribers to World is a disappointment to Kidani and the company at large. Unopposed by the WWE Network in Japan, World has more access to the wrestling fan's wallet and viewing schedule, even then drawing a modest 30,000 subscribers. Further afield, it's an issue of time, not simply money that prevents sign-ups.

Even among those that are subscribed, time is at a premium, and viewing habits reflect that. As expected, it's live streams of major shows that attract the most attention on World, something borne out by popularity ranking on the service's site. World also offers streams of smaller shows as part of their service. These are either house shows, or ones that are filmed for Samurai TV (NJPW has an additional broadcast arrangement with Samurai, meaning that the network has at least timed exclusive rights to a fully produced show with commentary). Often captured by a single fixed camera, these shows don't feature commentary, and while a lack of Japanese announcing may have little bearing on an English speaker's enjoyment of a show, the lack of production on these events makes for a weak response. Behind major event streaming, VOD archives were the next most popular item amongst those polled, and a three hour plus commitment for 'minor' programming fared somewhat more poorly.

Approaching a year after the launch of World, a stronger emphasis was placed on original content for the domestic market, with short skits and longer form documentaries. Due to the language barrier, these fared poorly with respondents, something that speaks to a larger problem with NJPW when it comes to international expansion. The overwhelming majority of pollsters felt that removal of the language barrier would draw more business to NJPW World, with English website navigation and subtitles or English commentary on select video content being the top two requested features. After a disappointing start in foreign markets, World adopted an English language sign up page, but even this was confusing, translation being an automated Google Translate powered effort. Navigation of the site itself is entirely in Japanese, and a dedicated overhaul of the service for international audiences seems necessary.

Part of the issues surrounding World domestically is that traditional models still dominate viewing patterns in Japan. Live broadcast television is dominant in Japan, and conversation about 'cable cutting' is only just beginning. Popular streaming service Hulu launched in Japan in 2011, and only reached the million subscriber mark in summer of 2015, after a sale to broadcaster NTV. Stricter controls from rights owners and networks means many Japanese equivalents to Netflix (which itself launched in Japan in autumn 2015) receive content sparingly, or late, while many more services are fenced behind strict digital rights management. Samurai TV's streaming service, for instance, is under the Sky Perfect umbrella, the satellite broadcaster going into streaming in a response to falling subscriber numbers. Yet in a bid to prevent customers cutting the cable altogether, Samurai and other Sky Perfect channels can only be streamed to computers, tablets or phones, and not to devices that are designed to display on televisions. This leaves devices like Google's Chromecast, the Roku, or games consoles in the cold, and similar logic, as well as a lack of development budget has slowed the progress of NJPW World apps built for televisions. That has a knock on effect on customers based abroad; the convenience of being able to stream to any device in any room of the house is an expectation of most services by now.

Ultimately then, the obstacles New Japan faces in the west are the same they always have been - language and accessibility. Advances in both have created a niche for New Japan. 59.2% of pollsters had their first experience with NJPW after Bushiroad's 2012 acquisition of the company, when major events were streamed on a pay per view basis, making them either more easily purchased or pirated. AXS TV meanwhile, were able to trumpet *World Pro*'s success for their network. It's a boutique audience in the west though, that is unlikely to grow without dramatically improved World accessibility and a more current foreign TV offering.

Capturing a broader international audience is part of the 'new IWGP conception' announced in the summer of 2015. This will see further collaboration with foreign promotions and more to and fro of talent, which could attract newer fans with familiar faces from products they already watch. To survey respondents who are already hardcore fans, however, 'preaching to the choir' with already familiar names is not as important as presenting something unique. 51.66% of pollsters were 'greatly interested' in a strong roster of Japanese talent in NJPW, while just 22.5% said the same of a roster of foreign workers. The 'new concept' could best be seen as a discovery system for untapped foreign talents, and a chance for learning excursions for dojo graduates then, rather than an opportunity for already famous names to make their way across and take the place of home grown stars.

NJPW have lightning in a bottle with Nakamura, but his presentation can be applied to plans for more long-term success *Photo:Yukio Hiraku/AFLO*

Of the homegrown stars, none are more popular than Shinsuke Nakamura. Easily the favourite pick of those surveyed (45.2% listed him as their favourite NJPW roster member, from Kazuchika Okada and Katsuyori Shibata), his work has certainly put him into the upper echelon of talent in Japanese fans' eyes, but he is a superstar abroad. The long autograph lines at international tours once reserved for Jushin Liger, are now Nakamura's domain. New Japan recognise that popularity, but how best to leverage it?

Nakamura, like Liger or Keiji Muto, who had arguably the largest international cache of the original Three Musketeers, has an easy charisma and comfortably stands apart presentationally from the rest of the roster. He is an instantly distinguishable character, who as one pollster put it 'has that unhinged charisma that characters from the '80s and '90s had'. Liger and Muto (as Great Muta) were also presented almost as comic book characters, literally so in Liger's case.

71.8% of respondents were either 'greatly interested' or 'interested' in the easily recognisable characters on NJPW's roster. That certainly speaks to the quality of the creative overhaul undertaken by Jado and Gedo over the past decade or so, and condemns the homogeneity that the talent had during the 'Inokism' of the vale tudo era.

Yet New Japan is not going to become a breeding ground for over the top cartoon characters in a manner akin to 1980s WWF, and nor should it. Every single individual surveyed ranked in-ring performance as either top or second priority when it came to watching New Japan, and while there may be the occasional stumble, the high quality of work from the roster at large is unlikely to decline. Interestingly though, a majority polled enjoyed 'in depth angles and storylines' in other wrestling promotions, while putting heavy emphasis (61.69% were 'greatly interested') on clean finishes to matches with an emphasis on wins and losses. It may be difficult for New Japan to reconcile the need for episodic storytelling that western promotions use, often reliant on talk segments and backstage vignettes, with the traditional sports style presentation it still carries.

In New Japan, cuts to the backstage are rare, interviews are carried out more for the sporting press than the cameras, and in a bid to quickly establish more western style traditional heels, crutches like interference or striking the referee have fallen flat with critics concerned that the medium is headed for self-parody.

An interesting parallel to draw as New Japan continues to expand globally is to the videogames industry. While Japanese produced titles dominated global consciousness in the '80s and '90s, the 2000s saw western developers step up, and a separate design philosophy outpace the Japanese market. As Japanese companies like Capcom or Square Enix scrambled, they produced swathes of titles that tried to ape American and European philosophies and target the same demographic, a move that fell flat as games seemed generic and poorly cobbled together. As Japanese gaming occasionally shows signs of the unique attention and craft that brought them to dominance, so Japanese wrestling should not forget its core tenets. Evolved from western customs, storytelling and working styles, Japanese wrestling has become its own hybrid entity, and current fans flock to that. Expanding its scope to new audiences will be a difficult task, and with limited but growing presence in hearts and minds domestically, it's an effort that has to start at home.

11

Return of the King

Togi Makabe, for years a reliable workhorse for the company, would see his efforts rewarded in 2009 and 2010. A G1 Climax victory in 2009 would be followed up by finally winning the IWGP Championship in May 2010, dropping the belt to Satoshi Kojima later that autumn. Leading up to his five months on top, he was programmed extensively with Shinsuke Nakamura, and the feud sparked a major creative shift that made the latter a megastar.

On April 5, 2009, Makabe faced off against Nakamura in a rematch from the prior month's New Japan Cup. Fans were beginning to be drawn to Makabe's ruggedness and fighting spirit, but his GBH teammates were still rule benders. The fans cheered Makabe over Nakamura, who worked in a heelish manner throughout, landing move after move on a prone Makabe, and paint brushing him with disdainful head kicks as the 'Unchained Gorilla' refused to give up.

Twelve minutes into the bout, referee Tiger Hattori was sandwiched between the two, leading to Tomoaki Honma's cue to to strike Nakamura with a chair. He passed the weapon to Makabe, who looked to finish the job, before Toru Yano hopped in the ring, seizing the chair and telling his partner that he would deliver the *coup de gras.* Then, in a wrestling turn as old as time itself, Yano went to strike Nakamura, turned his hips and hit Makabe instead, frustrated with Makabe's losing form and their Tokyo Dome relinquishing of the IWGP Tag titles to TNA's Team 3D. Nakamura quickly scored a Landslide for the win, and continued to assault Makabe after the bell.

It was a cliched finish, but a heated one, and saw Great Bash Heel dissolve over the next month. Makabe and Honma were left alone in GBH as Nakamura formed a new stable with former RISE members joined by Tomohiro Ishii and the Giant Bernard/Karl Anderson Bad Intentions combo. CHAOS was formed.

Nakamura would state that CHAOS represented the very essence of the strong style that had been forgotten in the wake of Inoki's departure and the sale of the company years prior. Nakamura, of course, in storyline and real life owed much to Inoki thanks to his upbringing in the LA dojo and being rocketed to a main event position in 2003, and now represented the legitimacy that had supposedly left with Inoki and Hashimoto.

Yet this was no return to his shoot style presentation. Nakamura didn't brand himself as a throwback character, but instead as 'The King of Strong Style'. Leaning further into inspiration from Michael Jackson, he would wear a red leather jacket and dance to the ring, performing a signature pose of grabbing ropes and arching backwards on his entrance like a pole dancer. In his matches he would merge Hashimoto's snug, legitimate seeming strikes with Muto's otherworldly explosiveness, adopting a running knee dubbed the Boma Ye as his finish.

In interviews and press conferences meanwhile, Nakamura acted as enigmatically as his pop star inspiration. He would change up the tone of his voice, and talk in disjointed sentences, often seeming distracted or in a different place mentally, before gaining in energy and finishing with a trademark yell of 'yeaoh!'. From visual presentation to speech and most significantly in-ring work, Nakamura completely reinvented himself as someone unlike anything else NJPW presented, and it's to no surprise that he and CHAOS, originally presented as a heel stable, would be beloved not long after.

The Nakamura and Makabe feud would extend into 2010, Nakamura beating Makabe to win the IWGP title vacated by Tanahashi that summer due to an eye injury before Makabe returned the favour to start his sole run on top. The CHAOS founder would then be away from NJPW's richest prize for more than five years, but would be held as one of the best performers in the company, if not the world, throughout.

Cementing his legacy was his performance in the 2011 G1 Climax. Placed in the finals with Tetsuya Naito, he had a tremendous bout with the high flier. Naito had strong performances leading all the way up to the final, and it looked as if he could be broken away from team mate Yujiro Takahashi and given a run at the big time. Naito would come up from underneath Nakamura, who dominated for the most part with knee strikes and a more considered pace. Accelerating, Naito would unleash a series of attacks to Nakamura's leg in a bid to take away the Boma Ye. As fans began to buy in to every near fall, Naito missed a Stardust Press, leading to a Boma Ye to the back of the head, and a second a couple of minutes later for the win. The G1 had been elusive to Nakamura throughout his career, and while he was very much an established name by this point, the victory was an arrival of sorts for his current persona.

Though Nakamura would continue his rivalry with Tanahashi off and on, he would be denied the IWGP title, instead becoming synonymous with a new championship. The IWGP Intercontinental championship was created as a vehicle for former WWE star MVP, a Chono devotee who opted out of his American contract to fulfill an ambition to work in Japan. MVP beat Toru Yano in the finals of a tournament on a cross-promotional show in the States with Jersey All Pro Wrestling. While MVP had a decent mid-card run in NJPW, he would leave two years later having never really been given a significant creative push, working multiman tags with veterans for the most part. Instead, the IC title was shifted to Hiroki Goto, and then to Nakamura.

Nakamura would make the belt his own, decrying its bronze and black design as resembling a 'ten Yen coin', and instead introduced a white and gold belt reminiscent of WWE's iconic IC belt design. From here, Nakamura would spend the majority of the next few years with the belt around his waist, invariably with high quality performances.

Concerns initially were that having a secondary singles title in New Japan would water down the significance and drawing power of a champion. The title would not be presented as a minor championship, however. With the American model of monthly large scale shows being adopted, the Intercontinental title would alternate main event status with the IWGP Heavyweight championship, creating breathing room for the likes of Nakamura, Hiroki Goto and more challenging for the IC title and the likes of Tanahashi wrestling for the heavyweight belt between having to put in a main event performance. Having both titles defended on one night would be a rare occasion, kept for shows like Wrestle Kingdom. Even then, the intercontinental title would either be given close to equal billing to its heavyweight cousin (at Wrestle Kingdom 9, for instance, when Nakamura faced Kota Ibushi, who was now a full time NJPW talent, in an instant classic) or even higher, as in Wrestle Kingdom 8, when a fan vote put the continuation of the Nakamura/Tanahashi rivalry on top of the card.

On that night, the IWGP Heavyweight title was contested by two former dojo classmates in Naito and Kazuchika Okada. Naito should have been cresting a wave of momentum on January 4 2014, but he wasn't. With a ready made story, he had won the 2013 G1 Climax. In 2011, he fell at the final Nakamura shaped hurdle, while in 2012, he injured his knee part way through the tournament, soldiering on and working hurt until the following month, when a breakup with partner Yujiro Takahashi saw him stretchered out of Ryogoku, taking nearly a year off. His 2013 G1 run should have been a star making one for him then, but he seemed a step behind some other performers in what was an extremely high quality tournament. He would eventually beat Tanahashi in the final in what was indeed a tremendous match, but by debuting a new submission finish that the fans were not educated toward and didn't react to (and that Naito would stop using soon after).

Naito's 2013 G1 victory led to a IWGP challenge that ultimately fizzled *Photo: Yukio Hiraku/AFLO*

Through Tanahashi's fantastic storytelling, and ability to play a heel to a segment of the audience, the match came across well to the fans. Yet reaction to Naito's victory was lukewarm, and after winning, he was programmed poorly. A run of high profile victories was dropped in favour of Naito chasing the NEVER championship.

Where the Intercontinental title was quickly established as a 1A counterpart to the Heavyweight grand prize, the NEVER title was more distinctly secondary, and with strange origins. NEVER had been established as an extension of the Lockup and Zero ideas, with a touch of the U-30 and Young Lion Cup concepts to it. Standing for New blood, Evolution, Valiant, Eternal, Radical (a mouthful in and of itself) the idea was for it to be its own promotion hosting young talent from the dojo and selected indies like Sanshiro Takagi's Dramatic Dream Team, Michinoku Pro, or Taka Michinoku's KAIENTAI Dojo. The promotion would run limited dates in small venues to get exposure for younger talent, and from its inception in 2010, highlighted Naito in the same way the U-30 belt buoyed Tanahashi.

The shows were infrequent and poorly attended, though, and the idea stalled before returning in autumn 2012 with a championship attached. On a one night tournament in the small Shibuya AX building which typically hosts rock concerts, indie workers both young, (KAIENTAI's Kengo Mashimo) and veteran (BJW's Shiori Asahi) were part of the 16 entrants, but none were allowed to shine, the tournament eventually boiling down to Karl Anderson and Masato Tanaka. Tanaka, then 39 years of age, won the title designed to showcase young talent, and would defend it on the NJPW main roster, while New Japan never again ran a dedicated NEVER show.

While the NEVER title would eventually gain a stable presence on NJPW cards after a reign by Tomohiro Ishii helped establish it as a title for a more rugged hard hitting style, in 2013 it seemed like a strange target for Naito. Tanaka, a fantastic veteran talent, nevertheless didn't have the main event name value that Naito needed in an opponent to beat, and the NEVER championship was perceived on such a lower level to the IWGP title that it almost seemed irrelevant. Naito beat Tanaka in a decent match, selling the surgically repaired knee before landing a Stardust Press, but reactions were still cool.

With Tanahashi winning number one contender status for Nakamura's IC title, an online vote was hosted to determine which of the Intercontinental or Heavyweight titles would headline the Tokyo Dome, and there was a landslide victory for Nakamura opposite the man Naito had beaten at the G1. While an inordinately long Dome show and tired audience actually helped reaction to the semi main over the final match of the night, it was a kick in the teeth to Naito, who would go on to linger in the mid card, despite some fantastic matches later in the summer of 2014.

Naito had lost out on his first Dome main event, but Okada had already had his time in the limelight, even in his mid twenties. After a poor run in the US with TNA, he would be made a pet project of mentor Gedo on his return. Reinvented as 'The Rainmaker' he would be a brash young and cocky character; a *nouveau riche* type with a loud golden ring jacket, and hip hop artist levels of bling around his neck. To make up for a shyness and deadpan humour on the microphone, Gedo himself would be his mouthpiece. Like a hip-hop hype man, Gedo would claim that Okada existed 'on another level' to the rest of the talent, and that he would 'make it rain' in every arena he wrestled in.

Coming back in January 2012, Okada would wrestle another dojo classmate in Yoshi Hashi at Wrestle Kingdom 6. Okada was roundly booed, and the match, buried low on the card seemed to amount to very little. Then, suddenly, Okada beat Tanahashi for the IWGP Heavyweight title a month later. The Osaka Prefectural Gym saw the young challenger knock one of Tanahashi's teeth out with a dropkick with height, but not the precision he'd later gain, before getting knees in the way of a High Fly Flow and flooring the champion. The crowd, witnessing a huge upset, seemed to have the air sucked out of them.

Fans were incredulous at the hot shot booking, Okada's aloof attitude, and his entrance just prior to CHAOS (where Yoshi Hashi would later join as the group's comic sidekick). His in-ring performances though, wowed audiences. Okada was taller at 6'3" than most of the roster, and incredibly athletic, landing beautiful dropkicks and diving elbows. His short arm clothesline finisher, sharing his Rainmaker moniker meanwhile, was well protected, and never kicked out of.

His defences against Goto and Naito made believers out of many who bought into Okada as a main event level star. In the summer, he would win the G1, beating Karl Anderson (only the second foreign finalist in history) in a tremendous main event. Anderson seemed to be headed for a singles main event run, having worked well with Goto in a brief feud when partner Giant Bernard was signed by WWE. The two gelled perfectly, with both men having finishers in the Rainmaker and Anderson's Gun Stun cutter that could happen at any time. The result was an intricate final few minutes that finally saw Okada on top, and an audience now fully in his pocket.

It was with Tanahashi though, that the youngster truly shone. The ace and the Rainmaker would work with one another six times in main events in the space of three years, each time with a different feel and an evolving story that saw Okada steadily come to be regarded as a favourite on Tanahashi's level.

Okada was new money, and was the perfect representation of a sea change that was happening behind the scenes. Yuke's had eliminated a lot of the company's costs, and it seemed like New Japan had a more consistent creative vision, but outgoings still outweighed income, with a calendar flooded with shows that weren't drawing enough to be viable.

On February 1, 2012, days before Okada won his first IWGP title, the company was sold in its entirety to Bushiroad. Fronted by Takaaki Kidani, the company was for the most part a publisher of collectable card games, with manga style cartoon illustrations. Much like video gaming giant Nintendo, Bushiroad was expanding from card production roots, branching into producing kids animation (made in turn to sell cards for their popular *Vanguard* and *Buddyfight* franchises) and casual, free to play video games for mobile phones. Kidani himself was a huge wrestling fan, having his company sponsor the 2011 G1 and running his own one-off show with independent talent that same summer; at a small 500 million Yen (roughly 6.5 million USD at the time) price point for the whole company, he jumped.

This was more than a vanity project for Kidani and Bushiroad though. He sought to dramatically improve the company's finances, with ambitions to have NJPW compete on a global level against the American promotions he was smitten with.

It lead to some promising shifts, but a lot of tension within the company, at least initially. Kidani slashed the number of events NJPW ran, from 150 in 2011 to 123, 112 and 118 in the following three years. Costs were brought down, and those shows the company did run were made to feel more relevant. NJPW talent was used to cross promote various Bushiroad products, many of which aimed at younger audiences. For older fans of the collector mentality, an NJPW collectable card game, King of Pro Wrestling, was introduced, and performed well.

In the meantime, Kidani sought to bring New Japan to a global audience. By bringing monthly shows to streaming Internet Pay Per View services, he was able to gleam at least some money off the top of an international audience that would have pirated the shows beforehand. As WWE embarked on their ambitious streaming network service, Kidani started his own with TV Asahi and NJPW; titled NJPW World, it even shared a price point WWE had turned into a grating catchphrase-999(Yen). Wrestle Kingdom 9 in 2015 would air on the service in Japanese, or on traditional pay per view with English commentary from Jim Ross and Matt Striker.

As positive steps that would see NJPW begin to turn modest profits happened outside the ring, Kidani managed to ruffle a few feathers with his influence on what happened in it. Rumors were already circling in summer 2012 that he was planning to put himself on TV as an Eric Bischoff or Vince McMahon like authority figure, which would have been a Beat Takeshi level disaster. At the G1 final that year, meanwhile, Kidani brought in two returning stars, to the surprise of everyone, including the people booking the show.

At intermission before the final knock out matches of the tournament, Kazushi Sakuraba and, more surprisingly Katsuyori Shibata stepped into the ring to a surprised roar from the crowd. Shibata grabbed the mic and simply stated '*kenka uri ni kimashita*' ('I came here to fight'). Sakuraba, having had his time as MMA superstar and 'Gracie Hunter' come and go seemed like an odd fit, but Shibata was outright inflammatory. Walking out on the company in the midst of a creative push, and his subsequent 'salaryman wrestler' comments led to much of the roster being hostile; especially Tanahashi, who had carried the company through its toughest years.

Kidani was certain Shibata and Sakuraba were of value, though, and lobbied for the pair being given heavy pushes, high profile victories, or even be paired with himself in a sports entertainment style angle. Jado and Gedo shot down the idea, instead having Wrestle Kingdom 7 see Makabe and Nakamura beat Shibata and Sakuraba respectively. In the subsequent fall-out, a church and state style separation between creative and business was agreed upon.

The compromise worked out for all concerned. Sakuraba, granted, seemed shaky at times, especially in a poor feud that involved him teaming with Yuji Nagata against MMA fighters Rolles and Daniel Gracie. Nagata did his best to carry some appalling tag matches, but it didn't work.

What did for Sakuraba were programs that harkened back to his UWFi days rather than his PRIDE ones. That WK7 bout with Nakamura, with extremely low expectations, was phenomenal, with brutal strikes taking precedence over grappling. A Wrestle Kingdom 9 match with Minoru Suzuki meanwhile was a well orchestrated nostalgia act, both men shaking hands afterward as UWFi theme music blared.

Shibata was still a strong in-ring hand meanwhile, and he had compelling matches with opponents that shared his hard hitting mindset. Successive G1s in 2013 and 2014 saw him wrestle extremely physical bouts with Tomohiro Ishii, the latter even more of an achievement as Ishii worked with a badly injured shoulder. He would work against, and then in a tag team with, school friend Hiroki Goto as well.

As good as those programs were, they presented a dangerous wrestling philosophy. They laid shots in incredibly hard, most significantly headbutts with absolutely nothing protecting skull on skull contact. Especially in the wake of the deaths that had occurred in the preceding years, Shibata, Ishii and Goto presented a triumvirate of unnecessary excess.

Tanahashi was particularly vocal about what he dubbed the '*bachi bachi*' style in his 2013 book *Tanahashi Hiroshi ha naze Shin Nihon Puroresu wo kaeru koto ga dekita no ka* (lit. 'Why was Hiroshi Tanahashi Able To Change NJPW?').

Goto and Shibata would transition from a compelling singles program into a tag team in 2014. *Photo: Nikkan Sports/AFLO*

He'd state concerns that *bachi bachi* had been bought out of a misplaced desire to appeal to fans of MMA by trying to appear more solid and legitimate rather than presenting something different entirely and appealing to storytelling and psychology. He criticised Shibata's approach as containing dangerous moves that ultimately meant little to fans' minds, as well as being heavily critical of his departure years before.

There was a very real dislike between Tanahashi and Shibata, and as is often the case, fans' awareness of ill feeling meant they were rabid to see the two lock up in-ring. In fact, this had happened once before; Shibata had briefly returned in 2006, hired as a freelancer and put opposite Tanahashi on the January 4 Dome show that year. That match saw Shibata go over strongly landing a barrage of unanswered kicks before pinning the ace; a short sighted move in hindsight, given that Shibata would again leave by the following month, and Tanahashi would shortly be given the IWGP championship. Ill feelings festered, and finally came to be played out in-ring in 2014.

In the G1 that year, the two met in a group match in Ryogoku, where Tanahashi rolled up Shibata to avoid the Go To Sleep Shibata had borrowed as a finishing move from friend KENTA. That September in Kobe, the two worked a longer form featured match. While Shibata still showed off his trademark strikes, the match had more of a considered, Tanahashi style pace. Tanahashi would counter a running soccer ball like kick into a Dragon Screw before landing a distinctly Shibata style corner dropkick and a High Fly Flow. While the match itself was entertaining, the real emotion between the two made the bout memorable, and both embraced in tears afterward, with the implication being fences had been mended. Shibata seemed to have been accepted at last by Tanahashi, and the locker room at large.

If fallout from Shibata's return caused Kidani to take a strictly business role, there were instances when his vision for NJPW's long-term profitability imprinted indirectly on creative. His desire to drive foreign interest in the product, for one, would see international partnerships bring wrestlers from Ring of Honor in the US, as well as the debut for one of the promotion's hottest merchandise tickets.

Prince Devitt was arguably the most compelling figure in professional wrestling in spring of 2013. An exceptionally talented junior wrestler, he nonetheless seemed to have stalled at the top of a thin junior division by Wrestle Kingdom 7, facing off in a three way bout with Kota Ibushi, who at that point didn't have a full time deal with the company, and Lowki, who was about to leave. Considering a departure to new pastures, Devitt was convinced to stay, and teased moving to the heavyweight division as part of a phenomenal program with Tanahashi. Trying to prove his worthiness of heavyweight main event status, Devitt seemed to grow ever more desperate in their series of matches, bending and breaking more rules.

On April 7, Devitt turned on Apollo55 team-mate Ryusuke Taguchi, recruiting Tongan NJPW dojo recruit 'King' Fale Simitaitoko as a bodyguard. Devitt and Fale would be presented as the arrogant smaller star hiding behind a giant of a man in a manner similar to Shawn Michaels and Diesel in mid 1990s WWF; to clearly define their roles, King Fale would hastily be renamed Bad Luck so as not to look superior to the Prince.

The next month, Karl Anderson and Tama Tonga would join Devitt and Fale after a rematch of Anderson and Tanahashi from that February. Devitt mimed placing a gun to Tanahashi's head and pulling the trigger, forming the Bullet Club.

The Bullet Club created a rare breed of strong heel heat from the Japanese audience in successive months. Edgy, and purposely against the grain of the Japanese sports style presentation of wrestling, the group would repeatedly cheat to win, before orchestrating backstage angles, using strong language that would get them very real warnings from management, and roughing up journalists. In the hotter markets of Osaka and Tokyo, crowd tensions were so high as to almost feel dangerous; fans would chant '*kaere*' ('go home!') with such venom as to evoke the nationalistic fervour of NJPW 40 years earlier.

The summer of 2013 saw peak heat for the Bullet Club, including Devitt's final Best of the Super Juniors victory, edging out Alex Shelley in the midst of a near rioting Korakuen. As we've seen in the past, however, the light that burns twice as brightly does so for half as long. Bullet Club quickly went from despised villains to cooler heels, who, much like the nWo, were strong merchandise sellers. When Devitt was signed by WWE in spring 2014, Bullet Club were already showing a self aware, humorous edge, 'paying tribute to' the nWo and the WWF's D Generation X with crotch chops, Wolfpack hand signs, and exclamations of 'too sweet!'. In a bid to counter any suggestion that the group was racially motivated, Yujiro Takahashi was brought in, though quickly joined by almost every foreign wrestler moving through NJPW's doors. Talented high fliers the Young Bucks, former WWE star Luke 'Doc' Gallows, nWo founder member Scott Hall's son Cody, all would pad out a bloated roster. Kenny Omega, a long time DDT stalwart, finally signed a full time contract with NJPW in the autumn of 2014 after years of freelance contributions. 'The first question out of a reporter's mouth at the press conference was "Have you thought about joining a faction? What about the Bullet Club?"', Omega would remark.

Yet while the concept might have started to feel tired to the committed viewer, the Bullet Club attitude and merchandise line continued to sell, and in featured matches, they continued to draw strong houses. It helped that while the stable was massive, most members played a distinct role. Young Bucks were a crude yet death defying tag team, while Anderson and Gallows were a heavyweight equivalent. Fale, with the right opponent, progressed leaps and bounds, and by 2015, with an impressive program with Okada, had grown into his role as a giant.

After Devitt left, though, Bullet Club continued to have strong leadership in the shape of AJ Styles. Styles had been a standout star of the 2000s in the US thanks predominantly to his work in TNA, where he was the focal point for years, and one of their few 'home grown' stars. After leaving due to a contract dispute, he made his NJPW debut on the same night that Devitt finished with the company. In Ryogoku on April 8, after Okada and Yoshi Hashi beat Fale and Tama Tonga, Styles ran into the ring and landed his signature Styles Clash on the IWGP Heavyweight champion.

Entering the company to no small amount of cynicism, AJ Styles blew away expectations. *Photo: Yukio Hiraku/AFLO*

Much like Okada on his return to NJPW, Styles would be hot shotted into the main event the next month, and like Okada, would win the title to boot. The parallels would continue as many were critical of a relative unknown to the Japanese audience, and one that wasn't working a full time touring schedule, feeling he shouldn't have been given the belt so easily. Like Okada though, Styles proved doubters wrong, with top flight title defences, and an astounding performance in the G1 that year. Against Naito, Styles would make the prior year's winner into the sympathetic babyface he should have been in 2013, working over his knee, and exploiting a cut to the head he'd received the prior night against Toru Yano. With Minoru Suzuki he had many fans' favourite match of the year, both men's approaches to wrestling differing wildly, and the Korakuen crowd being receptive to the outside Bullet Club interference's impact on the story of the match.

A slick gimmick tying together strong performers, the Bullet Club was a hot ticket both domestically and abroad. Where viewers of internet pay per view feeds, or NJPW World might have felt put off by the alien nature of the Japanese talent, unable to understand what they or the domestic announcers would say, the Bullet Club were a collection of familiar faces, speaking a language both in and out of the ring, that they were used to. They were a key part of Kidani's 'international appeal' tentpole of NJPW's economic recovery.

Another tentpole of Kidani's plan was, again, inspired by Western approaches. When cutting the number of live events NJPW ran, he'd also express a desire to add more significance to the shows that they did run, strengthening the brand of two New Japan concepts in particular; Wrestle Kingdom and the G1 Climax. Much like Wrestlemania selling as an annual stadium show on name value alone for WWE, the aim was for Wrestle Kingdom to grow into a brand in and of itself, with G1 as support.

The G1 Climax was quickly given more prominence than ever before, with a WWE Royal Rumble like stipulation added to the premise from 2012 onward; the winner of the tournament would go on to have an IWGP Heavyweight championship match at Wrestle Kingdom. The G1 schedule would massively increase as well; while previous years had settled into a ten show, two week format, by 2015 it would become a 19 show affair, held over an entire month. The increased pressure to compete in main event calibre matches on a nightly basis saw a series of injuries, but stars would be made in the process like never before, especially from 2013 onward, when shows were streamed online internationally. As mentioned, Ishii, Shibata and Styles all benefitted from the new format.

Tomoaki Honma did likewise. The former BJW star would take a leave of absence in 2012, after what management described as 'personal issues', but what many speculated was Yakuza ties amidst a funding scandal that was surrounding the further beleaguered NOAH. The leave was probably more at management's behest than voluntary, and when he returned, Honma seemed to have little direction. He wouldn't be booked in the 2013 G1 initially, instead playing substitute to a concussed Kota Ibushi. As a result, he came across as the perfect underdog, and while he lost every single one of his bouts, became a firm favourite with fans desperate to see his '*Kokeshi*' diving headbutt actually connect and give him a key victory.

Veterans too would see a new lease on career life in the G1. Moved down the card to participate in multiple man tag matches as filler, or ensconced in mid card feuds, the likes of Kojima, Nagata, and Minoru Suzuki would leap at the chance to wrestle long form matches and firmly establish that they still had value. Nagata and Kojima would receive occasional main event programs off the back of G1 performances, and Suzuki would be a mob don like figure, leading his own faction of Suzuki *gun*, which featured former WWE/TNA stars Lance Archer and Davey Boy Smith Junior, as well as junior heel Taichi, and Taka Michinoku, who had a similar veteran heel mentality and attention to detail that was a joy to watch.

The G1 would become the wrestling fans' highlight of the summer, and the start of a build to Wrestle Kingdom. In 2015, at the ninth incarnation of the event, NJPW World subscriptions, highlights on TV Asahi, and traditional and internet pay per view threw NJPW to an audience with a size and diversity not drawn since Inoki and Ali. Unlike that affair, WK9 was a phenomenal critical success.

That day saw 53 individuals appear before the crowd of 36,500. A small percentage of the 900 or so stars that had wrestled on NJPW's blue canvas, a crowd at the Tokyo Dome roughly half of what was being drawn at their peak, and all in a four hour moment in time that represented 42 years of company history. After a fantastic sixth meeting, Tanahashi pinned Okada to retain the IWGP Heavyweight championship. Okada, humbled, drained, would burst into tears on leaving the ring while Tanahashi preened and played air guitar for the crowd. It was a moment that encapsulated the thrill of victory and agony of defeat that is the heart of pro wrestling, indeed, sports, drama. The company had experienced both, and as it continued to turn its darkest corners, would surely have a turbulent road ahead.

Epilogue: Down the Tokon Road

So what does the future hold for NJPW? As 2015 wore on, company business was a mixed bag of success and disappointment. Live gates remained strong, Ryogoku being a consistent sell out, and the in-ring product was still for the most part very good. Kota Ibushi, who raised his game after transitioning to heavyweight in 2014, was stringing together a strong resume of main event performances. Against Nakamura at WK9, he had a spectacular effort, showing a more brutal side to his character and movements, while later that spring, he would challenge for AJ Styles' IWGP title in another amazing bout that saw best friend and Bullet Club member Kenny Omega factored into the finish before Styles caught a Phoenix Splash in mid air and nailed the Styles Clash.

The company continued to push international expansion as its key aim in the early part of 2015, and would often appeal to foreign fans with a large number of western wrestlers on every card. Events began to feature a number of bouts entirely comprised of international talent, which often left more casual live crowds confused and lost. Moreover, foreign talent that could speak Japanese and help establish themselves and their matches to the non English speaking audience, weren't allowed to do so. 'You'd think if they didn't (allow us to speak Japanese), they'd be making a big mistake,' the bilingual Omega would remark. 'As foreigners, we're kind of mysterious, and it's hard for the audience to know who we really are and what we're thinking'.

Meanwhile, young domestic talents were left to linger inordinately long periods before taking their learning excursions and returns as full blown characters. Yohei Komatsu and Sho Tanaka would appear to spin their wheels opening shows throughout 2015, working well with one another and the occasional veteran, without being given their big break; possibly because their senior Young Lion Takaaki Watanabe had been stationed in the US for close to a year receiving precious few bookings. After the NEVER experiment had been abandoned, and without a Young Lion's Cup or any tournament or angle on the horizon to get their teeth stuck into, the younger stars felt somewhat aimless.

Veterans like Yuji Nagata would also seem lost. As the main events were given over to younger stars, Nagata still had much to offer, but would instead be buried further down the card. He would contemplate retiring after WK9, a show that saw him participate in the pre-show battle royal for the live audience, but would stay, inspired by Ibushi's bout, to request to work with Nakamura. The ensuing match was decent, if outshone by a fantastic Tomoaki Honma/Tomohiro Ishii bout before it, but Nagata soon faded back into relative obscurity.

Nagata had a better time of it in 2014 working for NOAH. As the Misawa founded company limped on, NJPW would work closely with the group to keep it afloat, sending Nagata across to win their GHC title and hold onto it through a series of strong matches. Bushiroad and NJPW would gradually increase their financial stake in the company to a controlling one, and in 2015, Minoru Suzuki and the Suzuki-gun would 'invade' NOAH, making GHC champions of the entire group in different divisions. It would spark an interest in NOAH that didn't exist when the roster presented their shows alone, and Jado would also be loaned to help establish a stronger creative direction working alongside main event talent and booker Naomichi Marufuji.

For as much as it seemed featured programs in NJPW were dominated by the young and the foreign, it was debatable whether there was a measurable knock on effect on business. As NJPW cross promoted with Ring of Honor in the US and Canada in May 2015, it was the Japanese stars that struggled to match demand with supply at the merchandise table.

The international fanbase didn't seem too willing to invest in NJPW World subscriptions either. While WWE scraped and clawed to their target one million mark by the end of their first year in operation, NJPW seemed to have a hard time to reach their 100,000 target subscriber number by the end of year one, or to double that by the end of 2016, as Kidani had predicted. While the exact number of subscribers wasn't certain in summer, an educated guess would put the number at around 30,000, the vast majority of those subscribers being in Japan. Kidani would claim that attracting foreign subscriptions was a top priority, but a subscription to an entirely Japanese service was a hard sell to audiences that had plenty of wrestling in their native language to watch, and many in the US would have their fill as classic bouts aired on AXS TV in the States with commentary from Josh Barnett and Mauro Ranallo.

Prior to the 2015 G1 Climax, Kidani made some significant announcements that might well drastically alter the company's path for the next few years. In acknowledging the challenges behind creating new stars, Kidani unveiled the Lion's Gate project, a more dedicated approach to scouting new talent domestically and abroad, and again approaching the idea of running smaller shows for developing talent to flourish. In what Kidani called a 'reimagining of the IWGP concept' meanwhile, more would be made of international partnerships in the west together with more touring shows in East Asia. These would also see more international content appearing on the World service.

Most interesting was Kidani and Sugabayashi both emphasizing the importance of drawing in younger audiences and families. This tied in to using cross media promotion as a 'Trojan horse' - introducing audiences to the likes of Kazuchika Okada via Bushiroad's *Buddyfight* and *Vanguard* properties so that NJPW stars would be familiar to younger audiences if and when the company secured a more prominent television presence.

It was an approach that spoke to Kidani's philosophy that 'the in-ring product in New Japan is the best in the world, but our business practices are somewhat old fashioned'. As Kidani floated the concept of turning New Japan into its own publicly owned company independent of Bushiroad, the announcements were at once welcome, and alarming. More forward thinking approaches to business were indeed necessary. On the other hand, a potential initial public offering Kidani hinted at was of more concern. It was a move that that was either proposed because of Kidani's fandom of WWE (another publicly owned company that he made reference to several times over the course of his speech), or as a reminder that Bushiroad could cut New Japan loose from their books at any time and leave the company to sink or swim on its own. It would be a risky move.

G1 2015, the largest iteration of the tournament to date, and subsequently Wrestle Kingdom 10 seemed set to mark an intriguing time in the company's history. Balancing a domestic live audience with an international streaming one, in-ring quality with out of the ring promotion, name value with home grown stars, New Japan had a lot of masters to serve. We'd learned by this point however, that the lion was too proud to back down from a challenge.

Bibliography

Various results, title reign data from cagematch.de

MMA records from sherdog.com

Rocky Romero, Kenny Omega quotes from conversations with the author. Available from liveaudiowrestling.com

Puroresu Dojo. Tanabe, Hisaharu. puroresudojo.com

'Rikidozan shisho otoko 'jiken kara 50nenme no byoshi ni manadeshi ga gekido,'" *Shukan Asahi Geino* (May 2-9 2013)

'Tokyo Underworld: The Fast Times and Hard Life of an American Gangster in Japan'. Whiting, Robert. (Vintage, 1999)

Pro Wrestling Hall of Fame pwhf.org

'NJPW 40 Nen Reki' (NJPW, 2013)

Wrestling Observer Newsletter. Meltzer, Dave

February 13 2012, January 5, 1998, July 9, 2009, March 10 2014, February 23 2015

'The Forgotten Story of Muhammad Ali v Antonio Inoki' Bull, Andy. *The Guardian* November 11, 2009

'Journal of Combative Sport'. Draeger, Don.

'Hiro Matsuda Remembered' SLAM! Wrestling. Molinaro, John November 28, 1999

'The History of Pro Wrestling at the Tokyo Dome' Meltzer, Dave *Wrestling Observer* January 3, 2014

'Brody: The Triumph and Tragedy of Wrestling's Rebel' Matysik, Larry/ Goodish, Barbera (ECW press, 2007)

Tokyo Sports Shinbun January 31, 2002, July 12 2005

'MMA at 20- Blurred Lines- Japan's splintered origins' Arnold, Zach. *Sherdog* December 2, 2013

Figure 4 Wrestling newsletter. Alvarez, Bryan. May 1, 2006

'Shinya Hashimoto Dead At 40' Alvarez, Bryan. *Figure 4 Wrestling* July 25, 2005

'Severe Sports Training Methods Became Kaibutsu Over Time'. Whiting, Robert *Japan Times* June 2, 2013

'Bring the Pain: Inoki's Continued Quest to Kill New Japan and Murder its Wrestlers' Sempervive, Mike. *PWTorch* January 11, 2004

'Naoki Sugabayashi interview' Takasaki, Keizo *Shin Nihon Pro Wrestling Pia 2015* (Pia Mook, 2015)

'Tanahashi Hiroshi ha Naze Shin Nihon wo Kaeru Koto ga Dekita no Ka?' Tanahashi, Hiroshi (Asuka Shinsha, 2014)

'Uchigawa kara mita NOAH no houkai' (Takarajimasha, 2012)

'Tetsuya Naito' *NJPW Documentary Series* NJPW World/TV Asahi, May 2015

'Shin Nihon Pro Wrestling Dojo' *Daikozu! Gekiteki Before After.* (TV Asahi. Originally aired June 2, 2013)

'Misawa Mitsuharu 5 Years Documentary' (G+. Originally aired June 2014).

Rikidozan Hae-Sung, Song (2004)

Acknowledgements

Undying love and gratitude to my beautiful wife AYA for her support and patience while thousands of hours of wrestling were sifted through, as well as the cover design work

Immense thanks to my brother MATT for the art and support. Love and miss you.

DAVE BARLOW, JAMES WATT and CHAD O'BRIEN offered help in their individual areas of expertise, with only a thank you for payment. Here is a thank you in print.

DAMIAN ABRAHAM planted the idea in my head I could actually do this.

The following people also lent a hand, directly or not, and I'm immensely grateful to all of them:

John Pollock, Dan Lovranski, WH Park, Wai Ting, Rocky Romero, Kenny Omega, Francesco Libassi, AFLO, Moritsuna Kimura, Yukio Hiraku, Nikkan Sports, Camera Press, Rodrigo Reyes Marin.

Indiegogo Supporters

This book was made possible thanks to the support of more than 300 people from 16 countries on Indiegogo over a 45 day period. Their names are listed below.

Aaron Conway, Andrew Hickey, Brian Alleman, Christopher Duarte
Aaron S., Andrew McNeill, Brian Hoffman, Cole Campbell
Abdileyoda, Andrew Swinnerton, Brian Kline, Colm Ahern
Adam Callingham, Andy Clark, Brominguez, Connor Gyergyo
Adam Donnelly, Andy Gray, Bulmaro Hernandez, Conrad Seidle
Ajay Sameer, Andy Patton, Carlos Loera, Cory Barnett
Alan Gutierrez, Angela Stephens, Chad O'Brien, Court Bauer
Alastair Fildes, Anthony Tovar, Chan Chun Tat, Damian Abraham
Albert Yung, Anthony Tuason, Charles Hindson, Damon McDonald
Alex Convertito, Antti Närhi, Chase Chandler, Daniel Carrol
Alex DeLuca, April Roper, Cheo Serrano, Daniel Morrison
Alex Edwards, Brad Preston, Chris Blasko, Daniel Myost
Alex Kramarz, Brandon House, Chris Brennaman, Daniel Smith
Alex Pileggi, Brendan Creecy, Chris Holt, Daniel Steadman
Alex Sarti, Brent Davis, Chris Robinson, Daniel Yost
Amanda Traphagan, Brent Lockman, Chris Sims, Danilo Cuevas
Andres Cabrera, Brett Hapgood, Christopher Bird, Dan, Lola & Max
Andrew Benjamin, Brett Symons, Christopher Cunha, Dany Bear Mendoza
Dan Robinson, Don Becker, Greg Flynn, Jay Phillips
Darrell Boland, Donald Holcomb, Gregory Davis, Jeff Parker
Darrell Chess, Dorothy Roberts, Greg Price, Jeffrey M Day
Darren Chua, Drappstar, Hans Hansen, Jeff Xilon
Darren Lyne, Dylan Jensen, Hans Rudmin, Jeremiah Olsen
Dave Barlow, Ed Burdick, Ian Tandy, Jeremy Edler
Dave Cole, Eddie Burke, Irvin Alvarado, Jeremy Spillman
David Dunn, Ed Strickland, Irving Lagunas, Jesse Templeton
David Foot, Edward Burke, Isaac Budgeon, Jesus Valdez

David Force, Evan Speciner, Jacob Harman, Jim Fischer
David Forde, Evstrike, Jacob Hernandez, Jody Plante
David Harrill, Fech, James Drake Jr., Joel Dellar
David & Lachlan Barrett, Francis Lane, James Farrington, Joey Bay
David Piggot, Frank Fusaro, James Hope Howard, John Cavenagh
David Taylor, Fred Caprara, James Klug, John Mantikas
Deadtech1, Frederick Cholowski, James Albrecht, John Edward McGraw
Dean John Roberts Brunton, Gabriel Talley, James Peery, John Park
Derrick Ferreira, Garry MacKenzie, James Schanck, John Pozarowski
Declan Casey, Gavin Alexander McQue, James Starkey, John Service
Dennis White, George Deane, Jamie O'Doherty, Jonathan Butler
Diego Santos, Gideon Grey, Jason M Combs, Jonathan Gallo
Diogo Pedroso, Greg Browne, Jason Presley, Jonathan Turpin
Jonny Allpress, Kim Wong, Marc Doogan, Michael Loukoumis
Jordan Benterman, @King_Hippo, Marcelo Torrejon, Michael Oh
Jordan Gallen, Kris Lipscombe, Marcin Martyniak, Michael Spears
Joseph Kurtiak, Kristoff Campbell, Mark Colomb, Michael Zloczewski
Joseph Regalbuto, Kyle Blevins, Mark Handelman, Mike Butts
Josh Boutwell, Kyle Kingan, Mark Jaeger, Mike Desota
Josh Coulter, Kyle Davidson, Markus Herter, Mikel Hernandez
Joshua Bjork, Kyle Robinson, Matt Barr, M.J 'Sexington' Smith
Joshua Murphy, Laura Kuhn, Matt Bell, M L Corwin
Joshua Shibata, Lee Casebolt, Matt Fish, Mohammed Elomar
J.T. Holdren, Lionel Edmonds, Matthew McCalla, Morgan McMaster
Kahl Sebastien, Lloyd Pitiot, Matthew Suconick, Nate Ng
Kasey Douglas, Louis Dominquez, Matthew Voigt, Nate Ranson
Keith Lipinski, Lou LaCugna, Matt Kennedy, Nathan Lake Bradley
Kenny Ortiz, Ludovic Leleu, Matt Nielson, Niall Hallinan
Kevin Aldridge, Luke Bovill, Matt Pecolatto, Nick Bakewell
Kevin Bui, Luke Faith, Matt Reischl, Nick Mahmood
Kevin Hare, Luke Grigsby, Matt Ricco, Nicole Caputo
Kevin Miller, Luke Howells, Max Kary, Nigel Bridgeman
Khalim Husain, Manuel Delpino, Medow, Ntaf

Kim Williams, Manuel Garcia, Michael Coccovizzo, Omega Masks
Owen Traynor, Rick Fichter, Sean Carleton, Tama Flavell
Patrick Cortes, Rob Deal, Sean Garmer, Terence Porter
Paolo Chikiamco, Robert Cochrane, Sean Spencer, @theEricWilliams
Parker Holland, Robert Faler, @senorLARIATO, ThePorkTree
Paul Andolina, Robert McClimans, Seth Powell, Tiffanie Early
Paul Blocker, Rob Limp, Shaun McAlister, Tim DeMarre
Paul Hull, Ross Binder, Shawn P Stewart, Timo Balz
Paul Hurley, Ryan Clifford, Shelly Deathlock, Timothy Tse
Paul Jaissle, Ryan Porter, Sherman Lee, Todd Clayton
Paul Stedman, Ryan Sheldon, Sian Willmott, Tomas & Lyris
Peter Peresin, Ryan Stewart, Spike Lee, Tony Rudo
Philip Linde, Ryan Tulleth, Stephen French, @traskbryant
Prasant Reddy, Ryan Wodson, Stephen Hutton, Travis Yacovitch
Randall Nichols, Sam Hiko Stoner, Sterling Ortiz, Trevor Maine
Randy Osga, Sam Razo, Steve Moore, Wade Yenny
Remi Julien, Samuel Naughton, Steven Debono, Warren
Rene Fischer, Saul Hernandez, Steven Pritchard, Weng Choe
Richard Milne, Scott Bankes, Stuart Fraser, WH Park
Richard Shelly, Scott Barker, Stvncksn, William van Dyke
Rich Fann, Sean Davis, Sunken Treasures, Will Young
Rich Moulton, Sean Kiyoshi Tomizawa, Survo, W.V. James
Vincent Cima, Vincent 'Wilde Kicks' Lemmen, Zackery Olson, Zach Dunn
@2m

Printed in Great Britain
by Amazon

68794112R00126